Oxford History
FOR GCSE

Multicultural
BRITAIN

J A CLOAKE
M R TUDOR

OXFORD

OXFORD
UNIVERSITY PRESS

Great Clarendon Street, Oxford OX2 6DP

Oxford University Press is a department of the University of Oxford.
It furthers the University's objective of excellence in research, scholarship,
and education by publishing worldwide in

Oxford New York

Athens Auckland Bangkok Bogotá Buenos Aires Cape Town
Chennai Dar es Salaam Delhi Florence Hong Kong Istanbul Karachi
Kolkata Kuala Lumpur Madrid Melbourne Mexico City Mumbai Nairobi
Paris São Paulo Shanghai Singapore Taipei Tokyo Toronto Warsaw

with associated companies in Berlin Ibadan

© J A Cloake and M R Tudor 2001
The moral rights of the authors have been asserted
Database right Oxford University Press (maker)
First published 2001

British Library Cataloguing in Publication Data
Data available

ISBN 0 19 913424 3

Printed by Graficas Estella, Spain

Dedication: For James and for Jane

Acknowledgements

The publishers would like to thank the following for permission to reproduce photographs:
Andes Press Agency/Carlos Reyes Manzo: p.4 (btm right); Bridgeman Art Library: p.55
(left); OUP: p.46; Corbis: pp4 (top left), 44, 51, 66; Arthur Curling: p.34 (both); Mary
Evans Picture Library: p.8 (both); Format Photographers/Pam Isherwood: p.63; Format
Photographers/Brenda Prince: p.57 (top); Format Photographers/Carol Wright: 53; Michael
Holford: p.6; The Hulton Archive: pp5 (top left), 9, 24, 25, 26, 27, 28, 29, 32, 37, 48, 50,
56 (both), 57 (btm left); Illustrated London News: pp13, 16/17; Jabotinsky Institute: p.25;
Mirror Syndication: pp39, 40, 60 (both); London Metropolitan Archives: pp22, 76 (btm);
London Transport Museum: p.33; Museum of London: pp15, 38, 55 (right), 76 (top); PA
Photos: p.4 (top right), p.5 (btm left), p.5 (btm right), 65, 66, 72; Photofusion/Bob Watkins:
p.5 (top right); Photofusion/Sarah Saunders: p.64; Punch Ltd: pp29, 43; Rex Features:
p.4 (btm left), p.5 (centre), 57 (btm right); Chris Riddell: p.77; Sporting Pictures: p.79;
© D.C. Thompson: p.45 (btm); Vinmag Archives: p.45 (top).

Illustrations: Jeff Edwards: pp12, 30/31, 61, 62, 70/71; Julian Baker: pp10, 11

Cover photograph: Tony Stone

**The authors and publishers would like to thank the many specialist advisers
and experts whose useful comments and views have informed the development
of this book.**

Contents

Preface

Multicultural Britain is designed to support the coursework component
of a GCSE in history. It is suitable for coursework in all the AQA GCSE
History syllabuses. It also offers many opportunities and insights for
the teaching of Citizenship. The book examines the overall patterns
of immigration into Britain during the twentieth century. In order
to promote a deeper understanding of the ways in which Britain has
evolved, and continues to evolve, as a multicultural society, some
selection of material occurs. The early chapters are a detailed case
study of the experiences of Jewish immigrants from 1880 to 1939.
The later chapters focus on the experiences of black African Caribbean
immigrants after 1945. References are also made to the experiences
of other ethnic groups, including refugees and asylum seekers from
Europe, Asia, and Africa, towards the end of the twentieth century.

For each of the main groups considered in the book, the following key
questions have been posed:
1. Why did people come to Britain?
2. What were their experiences on settling in Britain? What challenges
   did they face and how did they respond to these challenges?
3. What was the official response to and policy on immigration at
   the time?
4. In what ways has the movement and settlement of peoples enriched
   British culture and society?

Who are the British?

The photographs on this spread show some aspects of the diversity of British identity and culture. Discuss what we can learn from them, and what issues are raised, about being British.

Denise Lewis wrapping herself in the British Union Jack flag after winning the heptathlon gold medal in the 2000 Olympic Games in Sydney, Australia. Black athletes have been very successful in athletics across the world. Some people have argued that this is because of social reasons – that a lack of role models and racist attitudes have prevented black people succeeding in other areas, for example, in business and in the professions like medicine. Others have argued that black people have been successful in athletics because of biological reasons.

Appleby Horse Fair, Cumbria, is an important and popular annual event for many Roma gypsy and traveller communities, many of whom have a tradition of breeding, selling and working with horses. Appleby Horse Fair is an ancient fair, protected by law in the sixteenth century, for horse showing and selling. It is also an important cultural and social gathering for many Roma gypsy and traveller communities. Since the Public Order Act of 1986 it has been harder to lead a nomadic life in Britain.

Sacha Baron-Cohen playing his comedy role of 'Ali G'. The producer of 'Ali G' has said that the name was chosen to deliberately disguise the ethnic origin of the character. Sacha Baron-Cohen, himself, is Jewish. Some people have accused 'Ali G' of being a racist caricature, while others have defended him as being anti-racist.

Young British Italian girls march in a procession to their first communion in Clerkenwell, London in 1998. Italian culture has had a powerful impact on British life, including on art, architecture, language and food, from the Middle Ages until the present day. Many Italians settled in Britain during the nineteenth century and made a considerable contribution to industrialisation.

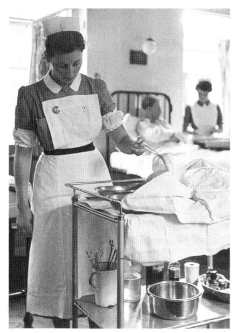

An Irish nurse in Britain in the 1950s, from an article called 'Why do these girls leave home?' published in 1954. Many, like the nurse shown, actually left in response to labour shortages in Britain after the Second World War, including in the National Health Service. There has been a long tradition of Irish immigration to Britain and the Irish are the largest minority ethnic group in Britain today.

Chinese New Year being celebrated in Soho in London in 1999. Many Chinese people, mostly from Hong Kong, settled in Britain in the 1950s and 1960s and set up restaurants and other businesses in the inner cities. The Chinese communities in Manchester and London are particularly large. Chinese people continue to come to settle in Britain today – many are refugees fleeing abuses of human rights in China.

Paul Boateng, Labour MP and Home Office Minister, has been, in the past, very critical of the behaviour of the police service in London and of British policy in Northern Ireland. In relation to his own life, he has written: 'One of the major problems of an MP who is black is to be recognised simply as a Member of Parliament rather than a black Member of Parliament...'

Meera Syal, who is of Indian ethnic origin, is a writer, actress and director. Syal is author of the novel Anita and Me (1996), director of the screenplay 'Bhaji on the Beach' and star of the TV comedy 'Goodness Gracious Me'. Much of her work challenges common stereotypes of Asian women as downtrodden, passive victims.

Rio Ferdinand, who was signed by Leeds for £18 million pounds, tackles James Beattie of Southampton, in December 2000. Ferdinand, who has played for England and for West Ham, was first signed up as a schoolboy in Peckham where he grew up.

 Q

1 Do you think these photographs are a fair representation of the diversity in Britain today? Why or why not?

What does it mean to be 'British'?

Since prehistoric times, different groups of people have been moving into Britain and settling. All of these groups have made important and different contributions to British life and culture. Some periods have had more movement than others and there have been many different reasons for these migrations, for example, wars, famine, climate change, economic change, religious persecution, prejudice and discrimination. What does it mean, therefore, to be British?

Activity

What can we learn from this Bayeux Tapestry scene about refugees, migration, settlement and conquest in Britain?

The numbered boxes below give information about some of the groups of people who have migrated to and settled in Britain over time. Match up each description with the correct group. The groups are listed here:

Celts	Angles, Saxons, Jutes
Normans	Jews
Roma Gypsies	French Huguenots
African Caribbeans	Bangladeshis
Russians	Afghans
Kosovan Albanians	West Africans
Irish	Italians
Indians	Irish Travellers
Pakistanis	Chinese
East African Asians	

1 Came to Britain from Europe from the Middle Ages onwards. Often persecuted and also expelled from many countries, including Britain. Up to 1858 they were not allowed to become Members of Parliament. They set up the first banking services in Britain and many successful businesses.

2 Came to Britain in large numbers in the nineteenth century, especially during the potato famine. Most came to build roads, railways and canals. They are the largest minority ethnic group in Britain today.

3 Came from a country that was known as East Pakistan up to 1971. Many came in the 1960s and 1970s and set up businesses, including restaurants and textile workshops. Their main religion is Islam and they speak many languages including Bengali, English and Sylheti.

4 Came from islands near the Americas. Originally they were taken to those islands against their will as slaves from Africa. Their main religion is Christianity. After the Second World War, many came to Britain in response to a labour shortage.

5 Most came to Britain in the 1950s and 1960s, although many had come earlier from the time when their country became a British colony. From 1773 one of their foods, curry, started to appear on British menus. Those who came in the 1950s and 1960s came in response to labour shortages.

6 Came from India to Europe in the 14th century. Started to settle in Britain in Tudor times. Often persecuted by other people, for example, large numbers were murdered by the Nazis. Today many are seeking refuge from persecution across Europe.

7 Many came to Britain in the 1950s and 1960s to work in the hotel and catering trades. Many also came to seek refuge from human rights abuses at the end of the twentieth century. They speak English, Cantonese, Hakka, and Mandarin.

8 Most came to Britain in the 1960s and 1970s because they were expelled from their own countries of Uganda, Kenya and Malawi and because they were also British citizens. Many of them were business people and professionals.

9 Most came to Britain in the 1950s and 1960s, in response to a labour shortage, to work in transport, textiles, and the NHS. Their main religion is Islam and the main languages are English, Urdu, and Mirpuri.

10 Came to Britain from northern France in the 11th century. In 1066 their leader defeated the Anglo-Saxons in battle and was crowned king of England. They spoke French. Modern day English contains many words from their language.

11 Came to Britain from northern Europe in the 5th and 6th centuries. Fought the Vikings before being beaten by the Normans in 1066. Modern day English is based on their language.

12 Between 1919 and 1921, about 15,000 of these people came to Britain as refugees because they were against the new communist government in their country.

13 About 100,000 came in the 17th century. They were fleeing religious persecution in their own country and came as refugees. Most settled in the East End of London and made a particularly valuable contribution to the silk industry.

14 Came to Britain from Europe from the nineteenth century onwards. They have been particularly important to the food industry in Britain. Words such as 'opera', 'stiletto', and 'balcony' come from their language.

15 Many came to Britain from Ireland during the potato famine of the nineteenth century. They are distinct from other traveller groups and have their own language called Cant or Gammon. They have been recognised recently as a minority ethnic group in Britain.

16 Came to Britain as refugees in the late twentieth century and early twenty-first century and are the biggest refugee group in Britain today. They were and are fleeing civil war, persecution, torture and other abuses of human rights.

17 Many came to Britain during the 17th and 18th centuries as slaves and settled in cities that became rich on the slave trade, such as Liverpool and Bristol. Some had arrived even earlier as soldiers in the Roman armies.

18 Came to Britain from Europe before the 1st century BC. Pushed into Wales, Scotland and Cornwall by the Angles, Saxons and Jutes. Today in Wales many people speak Welsh – based on their language.

19 Came to Britain as refugees in the late twentieth century and early twenty-first century. In the 1990s many fled their country during mass murders of their ethnic group, known as 'ethnic cleansing'.

Dis

What does it mean to be British?

In pairs or small groups, talk about what you have learnt from this exercise about what it means to be 'British'.

For example, does it mean:
- you have to be born here?
- your grandparents have to be born here?
- you have to speak English?
- your religion is important?
- you have to live here?
- you must have a British passport?

What other ideas do you have about what it means to be British?

Why did Jewish people move to Britain after 1880?

Thousands of Jewish people moved to Britain after 1880. Many Jews left the Russian Empire and Eastern Europe to escape persecution and find a better life abroad. Jews in Russia were often the victims of savage attacks and laws passed by the Government made it hard for Jews to earn a living there.

Jewish immigrants arriving at the London docks via Germany in 1900.

Source A

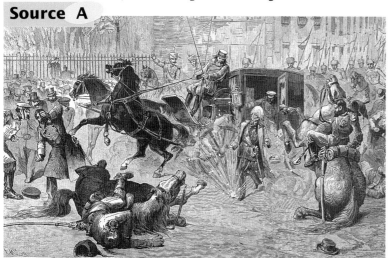

The assassination of Tsar Alexander II of Russia in 1881.

Emigrate Go to live in another country.

Anglo-Jewish A term used to describe Jews who already lived in Britain before the immigration of the 1880s.

A thriving community of Jewish people had lived in Britain since the seventeenth century. They had become a vital part of British life while keeping their religious and cultural traditions alive. Jewish people made important contributions to the social, economic and political life of Britain. Jews like Benjamin Disraeli or Sir Nathaniel Rothschild rose to important and respected positions in society. A small number of Jewish people continued to emigrate to Britain throughout the nineteenth century. However, most of the 60,000 Jews living in Britain in 1880 had been born there. After 1880 the small Anglo-Jewish community in Britain experienced a sudden and large rise in the numbers of Jews emigrating to Britain, many of them from Russia.

In 1881 the lives of Russian Jews worsened after they were blamed for the assassination of Tsar Alexander II (**Source A**). In 1890, the earlier laws against them were enforced with renewed vigour. Many became convinced it was time to move. Between 1880 and 1914, more than 2 million Jews left Eastern Europe heading for a new life in Western Europe and North America. Many thousands of Jewish people left their homes to move to Britain, where they knew that there was already a thriving Jewish community.

One of them, John Dyche, a tailor from Russia, wrote to a magazine about why he left for England. He said:

'Religious persecution was the direct cause of the emigration of large numbers of Jews. It was also indirectly responsible for most of them. In my own case, every day brought news of new attacks and new laws. I was asking myself, "Where will it stop? Whose turn will be next?" I didn't come to live in the fogs of England for the pleasure of it.'

A wealthy Russian woman, Vera Yureneva, remembered a time in 1905 when the Russian people called for change:

'Everyone in those days spoke of how dissatisfied they were. Russia was on the edge then. The authorities were nervous. They had tried to get people on their side by a war with Japan. It hadn't worked. So they tried playing the Jewish card. The Government always looked on the Jews as a pressure valve for popular tension. They organised pogroms [**Source B**]. At our estate near Kiev we had a servant who came to work for us after a pogrom. A crowd had smashed their way into her Jewish master's house. They grabbed hold of him and ripped open his stomach with knives. All the while they laughed and joked. They tied his wife to his bloody corpse and piled feathers on them. As she told us this story, the servant crossed herself continuously and muttered, "God will punish them!"'

Playing the Jewish card Using the Jews for political aims. For example, using them as scapegoats by blaming them when things go wrong.

Pogrom An organised murder and plunder, especially of Jews.

Source B

A Russian mob, watched by soldiers, beats a Jewish man during a pogrom at Kiev in 1881. (Jewish men were also forced to serve in the Russian army by the authorities, against their will.) One of the worst pogroms happened at Kishinev in 1903. Forty-nine Jewish people were killed, and over 500 were injured; 600 businesses and shops were looted and 700 houses were destroyed, leaving 2000 families homeless. The army garrison in the town did nothing to stop the violence and destruction.

Source C

The number of Jews in the United Kingdom, 1880–1921	
Year	Number
1880	60,000
1891	101,189
1901	160,000
1905	227,166
1911	237,760
1916	257,000
1921	300,000

Adapted from The Jewish Year Book and Census of England 1871–1921

Q

1 Plot the figures from **Source C** on a line graph. In which period was there the biggest increase in the number of Jewish people in Britain?

The pattern of Jewish emigration – young men, followed by their wives and children and then by older relatives – known as chain migration. Some then went on to the USA.

Source D

1. Jews may only live in towns, not in the countryside. Jews cannot own or farm land. Jewish landowners, farmers or labourers will be expelled from their village homes.
2. Jewish workers and craftsmen will only be allowed to live and work in certain areas.
3. Jews will not be allowed to own mines or work as miners.
4. Jews will be limited in number at schools and universities to 5% of all students.
5. Jews will not be allowed to train as or become lawyers.
6. Jews will not be allowed to hold government jobs.

It is estimated that under the new laws nearly one million Jews will be expelled from their homes. There will be starvation and congestion in those cities where the Jews can live, which will be a danger to their health. There can only be one aim of those people behind this persecution – the total extermination of the five million Jews of Russia.

In 1890, Russia strictly enforced the May Laws passed eight years earlier. This is an English account of the Russian May Laws, published in 1890.

Source E

In agriculture, the May Laws of 1882 did not drive all of the Jews from the land. About 76,000 remained but they had ridiculously small farms of, on average, 4.3 acres each. On these they only just managed to survive. As the law prohibited the owning of land, competition for rented farms increased, pushing up the rents. Farmers were extremely poor with few animals or farm tools.

Driven from agriculture, the Jews had to turn to trade. The most popular trades were tailoring, shoe-making, joinery, baking, butchering, and metalworking. All of these required considerable strength and little money. These jobs accounted for 60% of Jewish workers. With such a limited range of skills there was fierce competition, wages were forced down to subsistence level. The conditions of life were hard and precarious. Tailors earned 250 to 300 roubles (£25 to £30) a year, shoe-makers 150 roubles. It is clear that starvation must be the constant companion of most Jewish workers.

Jews were restricted from earning a livelihood in an honest profession. The numbers of Jews allowed in schools and universities was restricted. Sometimes they could only get a place when no Christian student was available.

An explanation of what working life was like for Jewish people in Russia. This article was published in an English magazine in 1905. The author was Jewish.

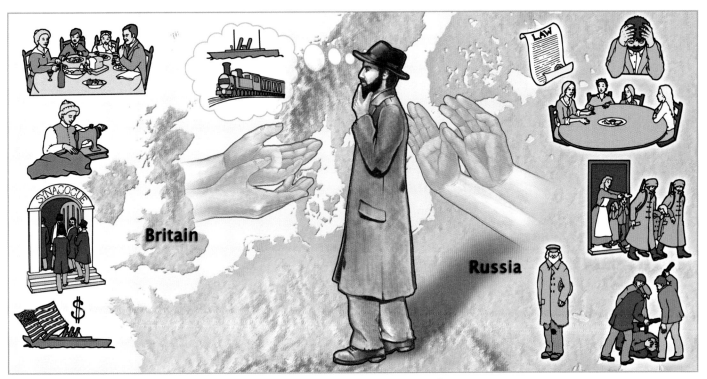

Some reasons why Jewish people left Russia (push) and came to Britain (pull).

Source F

The Jewish population in Russia grew and was restricted in earning a living. So an outflow of emigrants was to be expected. But it was persecution that increased the flow of Jews who emigrated between 1881 and 1914.

V. D. Lipman, A History of the Jews in Britain since 1858, 1990.

Source G

In the West, pogroms and persecutions were regarded as the basic causes of Jewish emigration. In truth, the picture was much more complex. The overriding reason for Jewish emigration from Eastern Europe to England was economic.

G. Alderman, Modern British Jewry, 1992.

Activity

1 Read **Sources D** and **E**.
   a) What was the effect of persecution on Jews who farmed?
   b) What was the effect of persecution on Jews in the professions?
   c) What was the effect of persecution on Jews in making and trading jobs?

2 Using the diagram about push/pull factors as a reminder, write as many reasons as you can about why Jewish people wanted to leave Russia and why they wanted to go to Britain.

3 What reasons are given in **Sources F** and **G** for Jewish emigration?

4 In what ways are they different?

5 Using **Sources F** and **G** and the information in this chapter, how do you explain these two interpretations of the causes of Jewish emigration?

How were Jewish immigrants received in Britain?

After 1880, thousands of Jewish immigrants arrived in Britain to a mixed reception. Some English Jews disapproved of the newcomers; others helped them on their arrival. The immigrants settled in the big cities, especially London. Many other English people blamed the Jews for adding to overcrowding and competition for work.

Where did the Jewish immigrants go to live in Britain?

The East End of London has traditionally been an area that has attracted immigrants, e.g. the Huguenots (French Protestants) and the Irish. As this map shows, in the late nineteenth century many Jews settled in the East End.

Between 1880 and 1914 about 150,000 Jews from Central and Eastern Europe came to Britain. They headed for the large cities of London, Manchester, and Leeds. In these cities were the greatest opportunities for work. In addition, these cities had established communities of Jews which the Russian Jews hoped would welcome them, as well as understanding their way of life. These Anglo-Jews lived in areas like Whitechapel in London, Strangeways in Manchester and Leylands in Leeds. By the 1880s and 1890s these parts of the cities were run down. The newcomers had to settle in areas that were poor and over-crowded. In 1880 there were about 46,000 Jews in London, but by 1900 this figure had leapt to 135,000. The two square miles of the East End of London housed most of them.

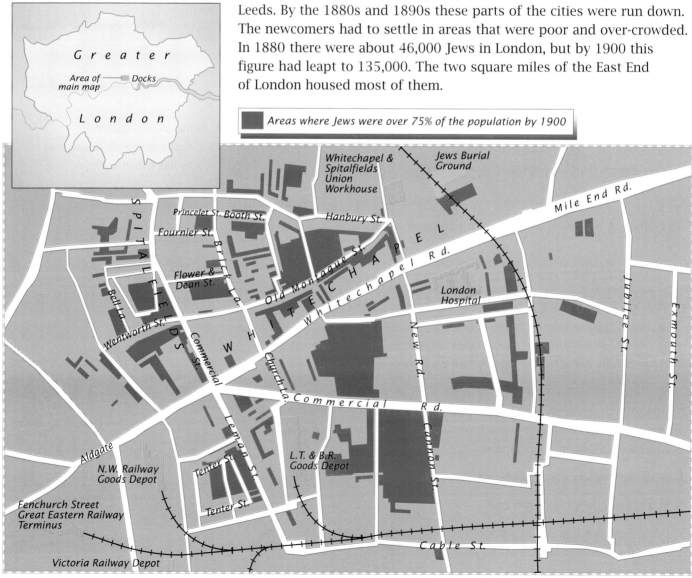

Areas where Jews were over 75% of the population by 1900

What were conditions like in the areas of new Jewish immigration?

Conditions were poor in the large cities that the Jewish immigrants first settled in after 1880. For public health reasons and profit, builders and local councils had been pulling down insanitary housing. This reduced the number of houses available and increased the overcrowding in many different areas. The overcrowding affected the Jewish, the Irish and English people equally. In London in 1888 there was an average of 54 persons per acre; but in parts of Spitalfields, around Bell Lane, it was as high as 600. Despite the overcrowding and poor conditions, however, rents were very high because of the shortage of housing. The cost, availability, and quality of housing were all issues that could cause racism and prejudice against the newcomers. In 1884, a series of newspaper articles focussed on the impact of new Jewish settlers (see **Source D**, page 18). In the articles, Jews were connected with high rents, overcrowding, and insanitary conditions. The pressure for somewhere to live led to demands by landlords or outgoing tenants for 'key' or 'blood money' as a condition of moving in.

The Jewish immigrants were not to blame for the conditions of the inner cities. They had little choice about where they could live. Most immigrants had to live in the cheaper, run-down property because it was all that they could afford. The few Jews who could afford to buy housing became landlords themselves. Jewish landlords in Leeds and Manchester were blamed for high rents. Overcrowding and resentment grew because Jews were more willing to share accommodation than non-Jews. It was also said that Jews were preferred above non-Jews by Jewish landlords.

The Jewish market at Wentworth Street in Whitechapel, drawn for an English magazine in 1905. The original caption for the picture was 'A street in London where no English is spoken – the foreign Jewish market in Whitechapel'.

Some Jewish people took positive action to improve their living conditions. Groups of wealthy and influential Anglo-Jews built 'model' tenement blocks. In 1885 the Four-Percent Industrial Dwellings Company was formed. Its founders, Lord Rothschild, Samuel Montague, Lionel Cohen, and other Jewish leaders associated with the United Synagogue, wanted to demonstrate what could be achieved. The company would firstly pay 4% interest to investors. This was a fair rate of return for investors that would at the same time allow affordable rents to be charged from the tenants. The second idea behind the company was that the flats would be large enough to avoid families having to share one room. The Four-Percent Company built a series of model tenements, of which the largest was the Rothschild Building on Flower and Dean Street. By 1899 the Four Percent Company housed 4,303 people in housing that had a death rate one third that of the Whitechapel average. In the 1880s the Jewish Board of Guardians repeatedly badgered the local council authority – the Whitechapel Board of Works – to clean up the area. In 1897 London County Council finally gave in to Jewish pressure and agreed to knock down and rebuild the so-called Bell Lane 'rookeries' in Whitechapel; tenements that had conditions which were amongst the worst in London.

Jewish Board of Guardians An organisation set up in 1858 by Jews to help poor Jews in Britain.

How did the Jews who were already in Britain react to the arrival of so many new Jewish immigrants?

Some English or Anglo-Jews were worried by the increase in the number of Jewish immigrants from Eastern Europe. Some of the leaders of the Jewish community in England were concerned about the impact that so many Jews from Eastern Europe would have on the good relations that Jews had built up with other English people. Anglo-Jews were also concerned at the prospect of so many poor Jews coming to Britain who would need financial help. The Jewish Board of Guardians tried to persuade Jews not to leave Russia, Austria and Romania in the first place. In 1884 they paid for advertisements to be placed in newspapers abroad warning that Jewish immigrants could expect no help or charity in the first six months of their stay in England. In 1888 the Chief Rabbi, Nathan Adler, wrote to his colleagues in Europe asking them to preach this warning message to orthodox Jews who planned to set foot in Britain:

'Many are lost without a way of making a living, they go against the will of their Maker in their poverty and overwork, and violate the Sabbath and festivals. Many believe that the cobblestones of London are precious stones, and that it is a place of gold. Woe and alas, it is not so.'

Other Anglo-Jews, such as Simon Cohen, tried to help newly arrived, poor Jews. He faced the disapproval of the Jewish Board of Guardians. A prosperous baker, Cohen had come to England from Poland in 1870. He set up a hostel at 19 Church Lane in Whitechapel, despite attempts by the Board of Guardians to have it closed down. A group of wealthy English Jews disagreed with the Board of Guardians and backed Cohen's hostel.

Q

1 How did Anglo-Jews help Jewish immigrants?

2 How did Anglo-Jews discourage Jewish immigrants?

Why did Anglo-Jews react in this way to new Jewish immigration?

By 1914, 150,000 immigrants had joined the 60,000-strong Jewish community in Britain. Most of the immigrants settled in London. Before 1881 London's Jewish population grew at 4% every year; after 1881 it swelled by 10% every year. The immigrant Jews also made a big impact on some cities outside London (**Source A**). In 1911 Jews made up only 2% of London's population, whereas in Manchester and Leeds they made up 5.5% and 5.8% of the respective populations.

However, of the Jews who settled in the capital, 120,000 stayed in the East End. This concentration of Jews in one place worried some of the existing Anglo-Jewish community for several reasons. It made Jews very noticeable in the capital. This extra visibility made it seem that there was a Jewish 'problem'. Anglo-Jews were pleased that they had made great progress towards acceptance and integration into British society before 1880. They were worried that the great number of new immigrants from Eastern Europe would focus the British mind on Jewish people as foreigners. This impression would be strengthened because the newcomers spoke mainly Yiddish and their customs, manners, and politics were very different from those of British Jews.

The large numbers of Jewish people in East London also put a strain on the housing in the area and made the overcrowding worse. Where

Source A

Jewish populations outside London

British Cities	Jewish Population in 1911
Manchester	30,000
Leeds	25,000
Liverpool	7,000
Glasgow	7,000
Birmingham	5,500

Jewish population in Leeds

Year	Jewish Population
1881	2,500
1888	6,000
1897	10,000
1904	15,000
1907	20,000

Yiddish A special Eastern European Jewish language, based on German but written in Hebrew characters.

An open-air service in Yiddish at a synagogue in the East End of London.

they settled, they formed self-contained communities with synagogues and their own shops. They printed their own newspapers.

In the 1880s, the leaders of the Anglo-Jewish community in Britain were worried. In 1887 a magazine of the time, the *St. James's Gazette*, claimed that: 'The Jews are a race apart. Long as they may live among us they will never become merged in the mass of the English population'. The Jews became news.

Scenes of Jewish life in the East End of London in 1904. *The main picture shows a tailor's sweating workshop, where the Jewish immigrants are both living and working. Around the main picture are scenes of Jewish immigrants arriving, finding temporary shelter and work. The pictures start in the bottom left hand corner. Can you work out what is happening in each of the pictures? This was drawn for an English magazine and the original caption was 'The alien in England: scenes of the foreign invasion of the East End of London'.*

Source B

What work did the Jewish immigrants do?

Concern about the new Jewish immigrants was focussed in particular on the type of work they did. This was at a time of rising unemployment and concern about working conditions. The majority of Jewish immigrants did work to do with making clothes, hats or shoes. Although a number took to furniture making, by 1911 about half the immigrants from Eastern Europe in England were working in the clothing trades. In London there were over 1,000 workshops. Most employed just a handful of workers.

The types of work that the Jewish immigrants chose to do – in tailoring or footwear trades – they did with other Jews, who understood their religious needs and could speak Yiddish. The work they chose either relied on their existing skills or involved skills that could be learned quickly and had a number of simple repetitive operations (as in **Source C**). All the work could be done in small premises, such as houses, cellars or sheds, by a small number of people. Working hours could be varied by demand or the religious calendar and the start-up costs were small. These trades had unpleasant working conditions. Workshops were cramped, unhygienic and sometimes dangerous.

The immigrants came to Britain at a time of rising unemployment. They worked only within their own communities in the large cities. However, British politicians and trade unionists blamed them for competing with English workers for the few jobs that were available.

In the popular mind, the immigrants and their work also became associated with the term 'sweating'. It did not matter that sweating had existed before the immigrants came, or that it existed in trades that the Jews did not engage in. The idea of sweating and the immigrant Jews became connected in the minds of many English people.

Sweating The practice of overworking and underpaying workers in cramped, ill-lit and unhealthy conditions.

Source C

Jewish workers making cigarettes at home in the East End of London in 1903, from an English magazine.

Attitudes at the time to the Jewish immigrants

Sources D and **E** influenced people's views against the Jewish immigrants in the big cities at the end of the nineteenth century. They present a negative impression of the immigrants.

Source D

So many foreign Jews flocking to the East End of London seriously affects the social and sanitary condition of that part of the city. The Russian, German and Polish Jews are huddled together in districts that are already overcrowded. They look down on the Western Jew as almost heretic. These strict Eastern Jews observe the Sabbath [Saturday] and thus can only obtain work in Jewish workshops. They are very poor. They accept starvation and assist the employer in defying the Factory Act, Sanitary Act and other laws designed to protect them. We visited one tailor's workshop in Hanbury Street. There was only one toilet, which flushed its contents outside the pan and across the yard. The tailor showed us his rent. It is preposterous that he should pay £68 a year for a house of only six rooms that is falling to pieces. In the top room 18 people were working. In the heat of the gas and stoves, surrounded by mounds of dust, breathing an atmosphere of wool particles containing dangerous dyes it is not surprising that tailors' health breaks down from lung diseases.

We visited Tenter Street and a Jewish potato seller who lived with his wife, five children and his stock of potatoes in one room measuring 5 by 6 yards. There was only one bed in the room. He was unaware that overcrowding was illegal. He complained about the strong smell of the drainage from the corner where a damp wall suggested a broken pipe. In one block of 39 flats lived 150 persons. Some rooms were so dark, candles were lit all day. Out of 15 toilets, four were broken. The flush toilet was so foreign to the inhabitants that they had not yet learned to pull the chain so as to flush and clear the pan. In Booth Street, 230 rooms had some 700 inhabitants. The toilets have been so damaged that they have been moved to the yard to avoid infecting the house. Now, however, the inhabitants, many of them foreign Jews, objecting to descending the stairs, simply throw the soil out of the windows, according to the practice of the Middle Ages.

The lives of the Jewish immigrants were suddenly brought to the public's attention on 3 May 1884. The respected medical journal, The Lancet, *carried a special report on a group of Polish Jewish tailors who worked in Whitechapel, London. The article focussed on 'sweating'. It had a dramatic effect on educated and influential people's ideas about the Jews and sparked off many similar newspaper articles.*

Source E

The Jewish island in the sea of English life is small today. But they will become stronger, richer and more numerous and get control of the Press as in Europe. Those who only know the faultless civic and social life of Anglo-Jews cannot judge the dangers which menace us as a nation. Six centuries ago Jews were, as now, the backbone of the trade in money. The English armies in France contained no Jewish soldiers; no Jew followed knight or baron; they grew rich and prospered at home while the blood of Norman nobles and English soldiers fertilised French soil.

Whatever an Englishman may or may not be, it is clear that no one can be deemed English whose diet is foreign, origin Oriental and when their ties with alien co-religionists abroad are closer than with Britons and when, for successive generations, they have proudly declined to intermarry with the people of their adopted country. Art, literature and politics do not matter to them. They have but one aim, making money.

Anti-alien Hostile to or prejudiced against those from a foreign country.
Anti-semitic Hostile to or prejudiced against Jewish people.

Arnold White, The Modern Jew, *1899. White was a right-wing social reformer. In 1890 he visited Russia. He gave evidence to parliamentary committees and worked to publicise his anti-alien and anti-Semitic views.*

A different picture of the Jewish community is presented in **Sources F** and **G**.

Source F

The Jews of the East End, whether from Poland or Russia, settled in where there is no work, surrounded by drunkenness and immorality in the middle of the dregs of our society. Whether they become tailors or cabinet-makers the Jewish inhabitants rise up the social scale. Often at the start they take unskilled work but soon gain skilled jobs. Why are they successful? It is because they value brainwork. From birth Jews follow a way of life that develops them morally and physically. Their religious laws make them healthier. The children of Israel are the most law-abiding citizens of the East End. They are peaceful, pay their debts and keep their word. The Jew regards manual work as the first rung on the social ladder.

In 1889 Beatrice Potter (later Webb), carried out a survey of the East End Jewish community for Charles Booth's, Life and Labour of the people in London, *1889.*

Source G

A report to Manchester council in 1903 about the poorer Jews there, said they were not diseased despite their squalid surroundings. They were no cleaner than other slum dwellers. However their children were well cared for, the community was almost free from drunkenness, there were few prostitutes and remarkably few deaths from tuberculosis. A 1906 study of Birmingham working Jewish women remarked on their intelligence. A 1905 study said that Jewish children were healthier and stronger than non-Jews because their mothers looked after them better. The Jewish children worked hard at school and immigrants were not regarded as a police problem. One police inspector said the coming of the Jews to Whitechapel had transformed the streets into places of low crime despite the poverty. In the East End poor Jews could find the Poor Jews Temporary Shelter (started in 1885) and many other communal institutions.

A description of the lives of Jewish people in England between 1880 and 1914, written by the historian, Harold Pollins, in his book, An Economic History of the Jews in England, *1982.*

Q

3 **Source D** is about Jewish immigrants and **housing**, **work** and **hygiene**. For each of these three aspects note down three pieces of evidence that the researchers identified. For each of the aspects say what attitudes the Jewish immigrants were said to have.

4 Which words and phrases in the article contribute to a negative and critical image of the immigrants?

5 **Source E** is anti-semitic. What criticisms are made of Jews in this source?

6 What different impression of Jews do you gain from **Sources F** and **G**?

7 Why do you think this is?

Many of the immigrants and their children went on to enjoy fame and success in Britain. Michael Marks arrived in 1882 and, with an Englishman, Tom Spencer, set up a company that by 1900 had 36 shops. Israel Sieff, a Lithuanian refugee, joined the company as a partner. Others contributed to the culture of Britain, such as the playwrights Harold Pinter and Arnold Wesker, the poet Isaac Rosenberg who was killed fighting in the First World War, the painter David Bomberg, and the show business tycoon, Lord Grade. The Labour politician Emmanuel Shinwell, later Lord Shinwell, came from an immigrant family.

How did the Government respond to Jewish immigration?

The Government responded to public concern about the numbers of Jewish immigrants by passing a law that controlled the numbers of Jewish people allowed into Britain after 1906.

To start with, most British people sympathised with the problems of the Jews in Eastern Europe. Two articles that appeared in *The Times* on 9 and 11 January 1882 explained the situation in Russia. The Lord Mayor of London organised a protest meeting at the Mansion House on 1 February 1882. Many important people, such as the Archbishop of Canterbury, Charles Darwin, and the Poet Laureate, Lord Tennyson, attended. Lord Shaftesbury proposed that a fund be set up to help the victims of the Russian persecution and £108,000 was raised.

However, from 1884 onwards, because of the numbers and prominence of Russian Jewish immigrants, some people's attitudes changed. They became more hostile. The 'alien question', which everyone understood to mean Eastern European Jewish immigration, became an issue in British politics. Feelings ran highest in the East End of London where most of the immigrants had settled.

What was the 'alien question' in British politics about?

The 'alien question' had three parts.
- Was there a need for control of immigration? Many people felt that a law was needed to decide who could settle in Britain. Undesirable immigrants, for example criminals, should be deported.
- Did aliens contribute to unemployment, poor working conditions, and low wages? This was the 'sweating issue'. As such, it was part of a wider concern about protecting British industry from unfair foreign competition. Immigrants, some said, were competing for jobs. The trade unions took an interest. In 1892, 1894 and 1895 the Trades Union Congress passed resolutions against 'alien immigration'.
- How did aliens affect housing? Some argued that aliens pushed up rents, and produced insanitary conditions and overcrowding.

Who wanted the Government to take action on Jewish immigration?

Interest in a new law to control immigration came from within both the Conservative and the Liberal parties in the 1890s. The Conservatives, in particular, proposed new laws on immigration without success. A change came in 1900. In that year the Conservatives won a general election victory on a tide of patriotic feelings about the war Britain was fighting in South Africa. Conservative MPs in the House of Commons demanded immigration controls. In the heart of the East End, in Stepney, a Conservative, Major William Evans-Gordon, beat the Liberal

deported Expelled from a country.
Trades Union Congress (TUC) An annual meeting of the leaders of the different trade unions.

candidate with a popular, anti-alien message. Following this success, he organised a pressure group, the British Brothers' League, to campaign for restrictions on alien immigration. He carried the same idea to Parliament, where he formed a 'Parliamentary Alien Immigration Committee' of 52 MPs, which demanded a change to the law.

What did Anglo-Jews think?

The British Brothers' League had some support from English Jews. Jewish MPs like Harry Samuel, the Liberal Henry Norman and other influential Jews wanted to stop the flow of immigrants. The President of the Jewish Board of Guardians and Conservative MP for East Islington, Benjamin Cohen, was known to favour controls. So too was the Chairman of the Jewish Board of Guardians, Nathan Joseph, who wrote in *The Jewish Chronicle* that:

> 'helpless Jewish paupers pose a grave danger to the community. They are useless parasites Many of them were never persecuted. To admit an unlimited number of helpless souls, who are mere dead weight, would not be mercy, but homicide'.

Government ministers, like Gerald Balfour, President of the Board of Trade, knew that America was about to stiffen its restrictions on immigrants. Balfour worried that Britain would face 'the full stream of low-class continental immigration' and needed to 'react in self-defence'.

What did the Government do?

With all these pressures from Anglo-Jews and non-Jews alike, the Conservative Government appointed a Royal Commission on Alien Immigration in March 1902. Its members included a leading Jewish figure, Lord Rothschild, as well as anti-alien campaigners like Major Evans-Gordon. The Commission reported in August 1903. Most of its members wanted to distinguish between different types of immigrant. They wanted to help genuine refugees and those who could support themselves but stop those who were 'undesirable', such as the mentally ill, the diseased, paupers or criminals. Many people assumed that 'undesirable' would also apply to those immigrants who were physically fit but who would add to competition for housing and work. A new Immigration Department could deport undesirable aliens up to two years after their arrival.

Lord Rothschild disagreed with the main report. He argued that the measures would harm many 'deserving people' who might arrive in poverty but could support themselves in time.

Why was the Aliens Act (1905) passed?

A new law was prepared based on the Royal Commission's work. The bill of 1904 would exclude as undesirable, 'persons of notoriously bad character, or without visible means of support or likely to become a public charge'. It was strongly opposed by Liberals led by Winston Churchill. He wanted to be MP for a Manchester constituency in which

British Brothers' League A group campaigning for restrictions on immigration. It was started in 1901 and based in the East End of London. It was backed by some Conservative MPs.

constituency An area represented by a particular MP.

many Jewish voters lived. The shipping companies who transported the immigrants also lobbied the Government. In the face of such opposition the Government withdrew the bill.

However the Conservatives believed that a law on immigration would be a popular measure with the voters. They had lost some support in by-elections and a general election was due within a year. So they made a number of changes and put an Aliens Bill back to Parliament in 1905. Immigrants could now appeal to an immigration tribunal that would have Jewish representatives. This time the Liberal Party also sensed that the new law would be popular and decided not to stand in its way. The bill became law on 10 August 1905. It appeared to stop those without money or a way of supporting themselves entering Britain. However, if:

> '...the immigrant is seeking admission to avoid prosecution or punishment on religious or political grounds, permission to enter shall not be refused on the ground that he does not have enough money or will be a burden on others.'

An extract from the Aliens Act (1905).

How did the Aliens Act (1905) affect Eastern European immigration?

Because the Conservatives lost the 1906 general election, Liberal Home Secretaries operated the law. They were generous in spirit and gave the benefit of the doubt to the immigrants. But the Liberal Government did not repeal what they recognised as a popular law. To start with, many immigrants were sent back on the ships that brought them, because they failed to state things that would have gained them entry or the immigration officials misunderstood the Act. Therefore, the numbers of Jews coming to Britain fell immediately after the Act until 1909. The message of the Aliens Act (1905) also made its way back to Poland and Russia and acted as a deterrent. However, from 1909 until 1914 numbers returned to the 5,000 a year average that they had been before the Aliens Act.

Many influential Jews welcomed the Act or refused to condemn it. The Jewish and non-Jewish workers in the East End of London reacted in much the same way because they shared concerns about overcrowding and competition for work. Influential figures in the Anglo-Jewish community had noted the effect of so many immigrants in one place. *The Jewish Chronicle* observed in 1888 that this: 'drew attention to their dress, language and manner which they might otherwise escape. Can there be any wonder that the vulgar prejudices of which they are the objects should be kept alive and strengthened?' Nathan Joseph warned in 1893: 'in 15 years the children of today's refugees will be the great bulk of the Jews of England. They will drag down, submerge and disgrace our community if we leave them in their present state of neglect.' To deal with this prospect, the Jewish community encouraged the education of the children of the immigrants.

Pupils at the Jewish Free School in Bell Lane in 1904.

Labour and the immigrants: What was the socialist response?

Source A

These aliens are chiefly German and Russian Jews who have flooded the labour market of the East End of London with cheap labour and reduced thousands of native workers to the edge of destitution.

From a report for the Government, written by John Burnett, a moderate trade union leader, in London in 1887.

Source B

The immigrants live on 2d. a day, whereas Englishmen would and could not. Seven Jewish or Polish workers will work in one room from 7 am to 10 pm on half a loaf. They are not careless with money. They spend nothing on soap, for instance, and their clothing is filthy. I do not think the Russian Jews are political refugees. Most have no political opinions at all.

George Green, an official of the union that represented shoemakers, gave this evidence to the Royal Commission on Labour in 1892.

Source C

To the Government, the alien question is a matter of locality and money. If you are a low-paid Chinese miner you are welcome in South Africa and if you are a millionaire you are equally welcome in Park Lane. But if you are a Jewish tailor flying from injustice and persecution you are not welcome in England at all. The rich Jew who corrupts our national life is to be allowed free entrance to our country, even our Parliament, while the poor but much worthier Russian or Polish immigrant is to be chased away like vermin.

The alien does not undercut wages and prices or take the bread out of Englishmen's mouths. The demands to exclude the alien are strongest in the East End of London. But elsewhere the alien problem does not exist. Due to racial hatred we often invent crimes and social evils that are really our own fault.

If love of one's own country means hating all the rest of the world, it is not only false to itself but also a positive danger to peace and civilisation. Who are persons of 'notoriously bad character'? Jesus was such a person to the government in Jerusalem! The Royal Commission says the aliens are sober and law abiding. What is an Englishman? The English race is no longer Anglo-Saxon but a mixture of the best blood in the world.

From a pamphlet called The Problem of Alien Immigration, *published by the Independent Labour Party in 1904.*

Q

1 What attitudes to the immigrant Jewish workers do **Sources A** and **B** share?

2 Read the following points taken from **Source C**. Which evidence supports each point?
   a) The alien question is only important in a small part of the country
   b) The government's attitude to immigration is hypocritical and contradictory
   c) Immigration can benefit a country

3 Use the evidence in this chapter and the sources to answer the following question: 'What was the socialist attitude to immigration at this time?'

How did the British Jewish community respond to the First World War?

During the First World War some people worried about the loyalty of British Jews and the effects of further immigration into Britain. This led to the passing of a strict immigration law in 1919.

How did the Jewish community react to the First World War?

The leaders of the Jewish community were very anxious to be patriotic and to support the war effort (**Source A**). Some 41,500 Jews served in the armed forces. This was 13.8% of British Jews at a time when 11.5% of the general British public served (**Source B**).

In the last ten years of the nineteenth century, a small number of British Jews, many of whom had recently emigrated to Britain, showed an interest in a new movement. This was Zionism. Zionists wanted the creation of a homeland – their own country – for the Jews. The favoured place for this was in the ancestral Jewish home of Palestine. However, many of the established Anglo-Jewish leaders felt that this movement damaged all their efforts to integrate into British society. They wanted Jews to be seen as a religious group that was loyal to Britain, not as a separate 'nation' without a home.

In March 1917 the British army invaded Palestine, which was then part of the Ottoman Turkish Empire. The British government issued a statement that broadly supported the creation of a Jewish homeland in Palestine. At the time it was intended to win support for the war in America. In Britain the Balfour Declaration, as this statement became known, caused great debate and division over Zionism in the Jewish community. At the same time, the British Government also made promises to the Arabs in the Turkish Empire about their independence.

Palestine The traditional homeland of the Jews until two revolts against the Romans in AD 70 and AD 135. These led to an event called the Diaspora or dispersal of the Jews throughout the world.

What did English public opinion think of the Jews?

From 1914, the anti-German hysteria that swept the country did not distinguish between Jew and German. Well-known German Jews were challenged to write letters of loyalty to *The Times* newspaper. Russian Jews should have been better placed because Russia was an ally of Britain and France. However, hostility to aliens did not separate *enemy* aliens from those of allied countries. Riots and violent attacks on the Jewish areas in London and Leeds took place from time to time throughout the war.

Source A

A recruitment poster issued by Lord Rothschild in 1916 to encourage Jewish men to join the British army.

Why was some English opinion hostile to the Jews?

Criticism of the Jewish immigrants centred on how many of the new immigrants joined up to fight. The Anglo-Jewish leaders wanted them to fight for their new country. But Russian Jews who had escaped from Tsarist Russia had no desire to fight on the Tsar's side now. This looked particularly bad when they continued to work while conscripted Englishmen were dying for their country. At tribunals, conscripted Jews argued that they did not wish to kill other Jews or that they feared they would be unable to practise their religion in the army. Press reports of Russian Jews moving from London to the countryside to avoid the Zeppelin raids added to prejudice against Jews. Anglo-Jews supported the British Government when it signed a Military Service Convention with Russia. Under the Convention, Russian men who refused to serve in the British army would be deported.

However, the outbreak of the Communist Revolution in Russia in 1917 stopped this agreement having much effect.

Two events in 1917 further influenced public opinion against the Jewish community. The Balfour Declaration brought attention to the Zionism of British Jews. Some people believed Zionism made Jews appear ungrateful to their adopted country – Britain. The Russian Revolution, too, helped form British views about the immigrants, many of whom were Russian. It was easy for the newspapers to portray the immigrants as communists. Many Jews had expressed support for socialism and the Labour Party. When the Russian leader, Lenin, made peace with Germany in March 1918, it was widely seen as a betrayal in Britain.

Conscripted This means being 'called up' and forced to join the army.

Source B

The Jewish Legion marching through the East End of London in 1919.

How did the Government respond to criticisms of immigrants during the war?

The Government passed the Aliens Restrictions Act in December 1919. This harsh law to control immigration meant entry could be refused by an immigration officer. Immigration officers had to make sure that immigrants had the means to support themselves and were medically fit.

The Aliens Restrictions Act (1919) had a powerful influence on reducing Jewish immigration. Zionism, too, went into decline. Anti-Jewish prejudice was widespread in some parts of Britain in the 1920s. The immigration of poor working-class Jews into Britain almost stopped. Using the powers of the 1919 Act was the Home Secretary, William Joynson-Hicks, a determined and well-known opponent of Jewish immigration and pro-Arabist.

In the 1920s, as some of the Jewish community became more prosperous, and obtained better jobs and higher status within British society, there was a movement away from the slums to new middle-class areas like Golders Green in London and Cheetham Hill in Manchester. At the start of the century over 80% of London's Jews lived in the East End, but by 1920 only 46% still lived there.

Q

1 Why were some Jews seen as disloyal to Britain?

2 How was the Aliens Restrictions Act (1919) different from the Aliens Act (1905)? (See page 22).

What happened at Cable Street in 1936?

In the Depression years, Oswald Mosley's political party, the British Union of Fascists, tried to win support through anti-Semitism. In October 1936 working-class Jews and their supporters fought with police and prevented a BUF march through London's East End.

Fascists Supporters of an extreme political system where power lies with a dictator and no political opposition is allowed. They are usually racist, as in Nazi Germany.

What happened at Cable Street on 4 October 1936?

On 4 October 1936, Sir Oswald Mosley and 2,000 supporters of the British Union of Fascists (BUF) planned a march through the East End of London. They intended to listen to Mosley speak at points along the way. Jewish trade unionists and communists organised a blockade of the route. One hundred thousand people turned out in the East End that day to watch. The marchers' route was blocked with barricades. Many opponents of the BUF clashed violently with police who tried to clear a way through the barricades. The BUF had to abandon their march from the Tower of London to Victoria Park in Hackney.

Who was Sir Oswald Mosley?

Sir Oswald Mosley inspecting his supporters in Royal Mint Street, next to Cable Street, in 1936.

When the Depression started in 1929, Oswald Mosley was a Labour politician. In May 1930 he resigned from the Government because it rejected his ideas for solving the problem of unemployment. He launched his own political party, the New Party, in 1931. After a meeting with Benito Mussolini, the Italian fascist leader, Mosley created the British Union of Fascists in 1932. They copied Mussolini's Italian Fascist Party. The BUF reminded many British observers of Adolf Hitler's Nazi Party in Germany. Like Hitler, Mosley also viewed the communists and socialists as a danger. He held meetings throughout England in 1933 and early 1934. He enjoyed some support from Lord Rothermere who owned *The Daily Mail* newspaper and made sure it reported favourably about the BUF.

What did Mosley do?

In the beginning, the BUF were not anti-Jewish. They had Jewish members. However, in 1934 the BUF policy changed. Jewish members were 'frozen out' and new ones discouraged. Anti-Semitic propaganda became a central feature of BUF policy. In the East End, the BUF tapped into the 'street-level' anti-Semitism left over from the days of the British Brothers' League. This feeling could easily be stirred up and Mosley gave it a middle-class and well-financed leadership. BUF campaigns concentrated on Jewish employers, shopkeepers and landlords. They said that Jewish employers were hostile to trade unions and criticised

Jewish shopkeepers for Sunday trading. From 1933 there were cases of physical violence against Jews, vandalism of synagogues and bricks thrown through Jewish windows. From 1934, there were a series of anti-Jewish street meetings. Jewish people were provoked and attacked. There was anti-Jewish hooliganism in the East End of London and in parts of Leeds and Manchester. The leaders of the Jewish community always said that Jews should not confront the Fascists. It only gave them publicity and allowed the BUF to say that the Jews were denying them free speech. Above all, Jews should not be seen as lawbreakers. A significant incident happened at a BUF meeting attended by 12,000 people at Olympia on 7 June 1934. Communist hecklers interrupted the meeting. BUF stewards set upon them with knives and knuckle-dusters before throwing them out.

What happened to Mosley and the BUF after Cable Street?

Immediately after Cable Street, support for the Fascists rose. However, in the long term the BUF were in decline. The violence at the Olympia meeting in June 1934 had already alienated many potential followers, particularly influential people like Lord Rothermere. The British did not seem to favour the militaristic style of the fascists. Cable Street and Mosley's other attempts to stir up violence against Jews amongst workers in the East End of London were much criticised. All of these things produced unfavourable comparisons with Germany. The Government clamped down on the BUF activities by passing the Incitement to Disaffection Act in November 1934 and a new Public Order Act in 1936 which affected the wearing of political uniforms and the holding of marches. The BUF never won any local or general election seats and was banned in 1940. Mosley was imprisoned from 1940 to 1943 in the interests of national security.

Police break down a barricade and force back protestors during the disturbances at Cable Street in October 1936.

Why is Cable Street important?

Cable Street showed that many Jews did not have confidence in the police. There were some pro-Jewish senior police officers but many Jews believed the lower ranks of the police force had anti-Semitic attitudes. At Cable Street, Jews resented the apparent purpose of the police to protect the BUF's right to insult and provoke Jews in the East End.

Cable Street also shows that there were divisions in the Jewish community. Thousands of working-class Jews rejected calls from their leaders to stay off the streets.

Cable Street proved to the Government the threat to law and order posed by extreme parties. They acted quickly to stop their influence.

1 What did Oswald Mosley and the BUF try to achieve?

2 Why did Mosley and the BUF fail?

Discuss

Were the opponents of the BUF right to fight back?

Why did people come to Britain after the Second World War?

There were two main reasons why people came to Britain after 1945. They came either as refugees from the war in Europe or they came from the British colonies and Commonwealth to find work. At first the British Government welcomed both these groups, mainly because there was a labour shortage in Britain after the war and during the 1950s.

Colony A country or group of people ruled by another country.

Commonwealth A group of countries that used to belong to the British Empire and became independent.

Cold War A struggle for power and influence in the world that took place between communist Russia and capitalist America between the Second World War and the end of the 1980s.

Old Commonwealth Countries that became independent from the British Empire before 1945, e.g. Australia.

Why were there refugees in Europe after the Second World War?

In 1945, when the Second World War ended, Europe was a very different place from six years earlier. Millions of people had lost their homes because of bombing or had fled in fear for their lives. Towns and cities had been devastated. A Cold War now began between communist Eastern Europe and the capitalist countries of Western Europe, as well as the USA. Countries in Eastern Europe were taken over by communist governments with very different ideas about equality and freedom to those governments in the West. Many people in Eastern Europe did not want to live under a communist government. As a result of both the Second World War and the Cold War, millions of people became refugees.

The largest of the refugee groups to settle in Britain after 1945 was Polish. Many Poles were already in Britain when the war ended. After Hitler invaded and defeated Poland in 1939, one million Poles left Poland. Many came to Britain to continue the fight against Germany (**Source A**). When Poland became communist in 1945, many of them decided to stay in Britain.

Why did Britain need workers?

Some of the refugees from Europe came to Britain in search of a new life and were welcomed by the British Government. Britain needed to be rebuilt after the devastation of the war. It was a huge task. Large numbers of workers were needed, especially in agriculture, mining, engineering, transport, and building. However, many British men and women had been killed and injured in the war, both at the Front and in bombing raids at home. Also, many troops were still overseas and were not 'demobbed' until several years after the end of the war. During the war itself, married women had been encouraged to work but after the war they were encouraged to stay at home with their families. This trend meant that even more workers were needed to replace them. The problem was made worse by British people leaving Britain to live in the Old Commonwealth countries of Australia, Canada, South Africa, and New Zealand. Britain was short of workers.

Source A

During the Battle of Britain, Polish pilots shot down more than 10% of the German planes brought down during the battle. They flew Spitfires or Hurricanes like the ones shown.

What was the role of the British Empire during the Second World War and after?

During the Second World War the British Empire was vital to the British war effort. The Empire had people, raw materials and industries that could all be used to help win the war. For example, two and a half million Indian troops volunteered to serve in the British forces. Between 1939 and 1945 India produced an estimated £287 million worth of war materials, such as guns and ammunition.

After the Second World War, the people of the Empire and Commonwealth continued to be a vital resource for Britain. The British Government encouraged people from British colonies to come and settle in Britain. This was because the problem of Britain's post-war labour shortage could not be solved by European refugees alone. During the 1950s, British companies and the Government advertised for workers in the New Commonwealth countries of the Caribbean, India, and Pakistan, as well as the Republic of Ireland. Advertisements were sent out for many different workers including nurses, doctors, bus drivers, cleaners, and builders. Many of these advertisements promised a friendly welcome in Britain – the 'mother country'.

Many people who responded to the advertisements believed that life in Britain would give them new opportunities to earn money, as well as being an exciting opportunity to change their lives. Lloyd Miller came to Britain from Jamaica in 1949 and worked as a builder in Notting Hill. He gave these reasons for emigrating:

'If you could make a few shillings for yourself, then you were alright, but if you couldn't make it, it was very hard. See, so that's the reason why I said to myself, I don't want to stop here to grow old and, you know, I want to travel and make something of myself...'

All citizens of British colonies, like Lloyd Miller, had the right to come and settle in Britain. When the Second World War ended in 1945, one quarter of the world's population had the right to live and work in Britain! This was because the British Empire had been so large. In 1948 the British Nationality Act was passed. This Act gave all citizens of British colonies and of the Commonwealth equal rights of citizenship with those people born and already living in Britain.

Source B

" So our poor old Empire is alone in the world."
"Aye, we are – the whole five hundred million of us."

A cartoon published in Britain after the evacuation from Dunkirk and the defeat of Britain's ally France, during the Second World War.

Q

1 What message is **Source B** trying to make about the British Empire?

2 Why were there so many refugees in Europe after 1945?

3 Why was there a labour shortage in Britain after 1945?

4 What were the two main reasons why people came to Britain after 1945?

5 It has been said that the Second World War could not have been won without the British Empire. Find three points that support this view.

Immigration into Britain 1945-1958: The big picture

Ireland
During the Second World War, the Irish Free State was neutral. However, about 60,000 Irish chose to fight for Britain. From 1950, Irish people were encouraged to come to Britain because of the labour shortage. Many were willing to emigrate to Britain because of poverty and hardship at home. By 1959, the number of people of Irish origin settled in Britain had risen to nearly one million.

Canada

Ireland

Jamaica

Barbados

Trinidad

Gambia

Sierra Leone

Ghana

Nig

The West Indies
The West Indies, a group of islands in the Caribbean Sea, had been colonised by the British, French, Spanish, and Dutch since the 1600s. The main wave of emigration to Britain from the West Indies was between 1948 and 1971. During the 1950s, people from the Caribbean colonies of Jamaica, Barbados, and Trinidad were encouraged to come to Britain because of the labour shortage. Many came because of unemployment and poverty at home.

West Africa
The countries of British West Africa (now Nigeria, Gambia, Sierra Leone, and Ghana) gave huge support to the war effort. They provided troops, labourers, raw materials, and naval and air bases. After 1948, West Africans came to Britain in increasing numbers. Most came to get an education that was not available to them in their colonised countries.

Activity

1 Make a rough sketch of the map of the world. Add the boxed information to it. You should write out the information from the boxes in note form. This will mean selecting the important points from the information given. Match the countries or areas to the map using arrows or colours.

2 Use the information on page 28 to add an information box for Poland. Select your information carefully and write it in note form.

3 In the same period, thousands of British emigrated to the Old Commonwealth countries of Canada, Australia, New Zealand, and South Africa. Add arrows and captions to your map to show this emigration.

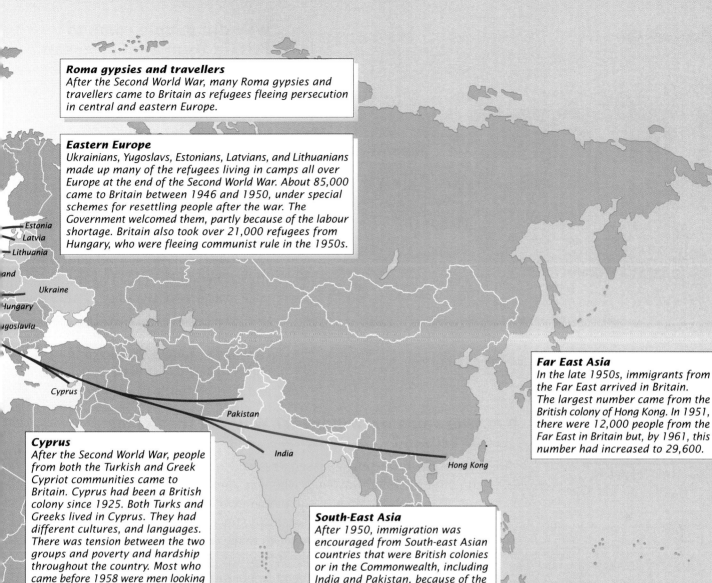

Roma gypsies and travellers
After the Second World War, many Roma gypsies and travellers came to Britain as refugees fleeing persecution in central and eastern Europe.

Eastern Europe
Ukrainians, Yugoslavs, Estonians, Latvians, and Lithuanians made up many of the refugees living in camps all over Europe at the end of the Second World War. About 85,000 came to Britain between 1946 and 1950, under special schemes for resettling people after the war. The Government welcomed them, partly because of the labour shortage. Britain also took over 21,000 refugees from Hungary, who were fleeing communist rule in the 1950s.

Estonia
Latvia
Lithuania
and
Ukraine
Hungary
ugoslavia
Cyprus
Pakistan
India
Hong Kong

Far East Asia
In the late 1950s, immigrants from the Far East arrived in Britain. The largest number came from the British colony of Hong Kong. In 1951, there were 12,000 people from the Far East in Britain but, by 1961, this number had increased to 29,600.

Cyprus
After the Second World War, people from both the Turkish and Greek Cypriot communities came to Britain. Cyprus had been a British colony since 1925. Both Turks and Greeks lived in Cyprus. They had different cultures, and languages. There was tension between the two groups and poverty and hardship throughout the country. Most who came before 1958 were men looking for work or families joining men who had come before the war. Some came to escape the difficult political situation in Cyprus.

South-East Asia
After 1950, immigration was encouraged from South-east Asian countries that were British colonies or in the Commonwealth, including India and Pakistan, because of the labour shortage. After the partition of India into India and Pakistan in 1947, many found themselves homeless. By 1958 about 55,000 Indians and Pakistanis had come to Britain.

Australia

South
Africa

New
Zealand

Source C

Caribbean immigrants arrive at Southampton in 1956.

Q

6 Look closely at **Source C.**
  a) What do you think is happening in this photograph?
  b) What do you notice about the people?
  c) Why do you think they are wearing smart clothes?
  d) Why are there so many men and so few women?
  e) Why are there no children?
  After finishing this chapter you should have more ideas.

Source D

Well, the average Jamaican who came on Windrush was not poor. The poor man did not have £28.10. In my case, it cost three cows. And I think you'll find the other passengers were people like myself, looking for hope, betterment. Yes, one or two might be unemployed but they were from a family background of support. So, they were above average as far as income was concerned.

Quoted in M. Phillips and T. Phillips, Windrush, *1998.*

Why did people come to Britain from the Caribbean after 1945?

On 22 June 1948, 492 Jamaicans walked off a ship called *Windrush* in Tilbury on the River Thames into a new life in Britain. Journalists, politicians and celebrities were waiting to greet them. A film was made of their arrival and shown in cinemas across Britain. The headline of the *Evening Standard* newspaper read 'WELCOME HOME' and the *Daily Worker* newspaper called its front-page article 'FIVE HUNDRED PAIRS OF WILLING HANDS'. However, not everyone was so welcoming. In Parliament, some MPs started to worry about the arrival of these Jamaicans and to refer to them as a 'problem'.

Who came on *Windrush*? Why did they come to Britain?

One of the few women passengers on *Windrush*, Lucile Harris, was coming to join her husband, who was already living in Britain. Lucile was an exception. Most of the passengers were young men in their twenties. Very few of them meant to stay in Britain for more than a few years. They came for adventure, to make money, to visit relatives and to see the world. Although most planned to make some money and then go home, very few of them ever returned to the Caribbean to live. As one *Windrush* passenger recalled:

> 'ninety nine out of a hundred had the same idea, that they're not coming over here into this cold country to live for ever; a short period, get some money, go back home. But it never happened... they're still here because they never earn enough to enable them to go home...'

The cost of the fare to travel on *Windrush* was £28.10 – a lot of money in 1948, as *Windrush* passenger Sam King remembers in **Source D**.

The people who came on *Windrush* attracted the attention of film-makers, newspapers and politicians because they were doing something new. There had been a small number of black Caribbean people living in Britain since Tudor times. However, the main period of immigration of black Caribbean people into Britain started with the arrival of *Windrush* in 1948 and continued throughout the 1950s.

Emigration from the Caribbean to other countries was not a new development – people had been emigrating from the Caribbean to the USA and Central America long before the Second World War. What was different after 1948 was that people came to Britain as well as going to other countries. This change happened partly because of the Second World War. During the war, thousands of Caribbean men and women had been recruited into the British armed forces. Some of them had served in Britain and wanted to return there. Some were curious to see the country that they had fought for.

Why did so many people emigrate to Britain from the Caribbean during the 1950s?

At first, very few people came to England from the Caribbean. However, the destruction caused by a hurricane in Jamaica in 1951 increased the pace of emigration. In 1952 immigration into the USA was heavily restricted and people from the Caribbean who wished to emigrate had to look elsewhere. At the same time employers in Britain realised that if they were going to fill all their job vacancies, they needed to work harder to recruit more workers from other countries. Companies such as the British Hotels and Restaurants Association set up offices in Jamaica and Barbados to recruit skilled staff. London Transport loaned the cost of fares to Britain to people who were willing to take up jobs.

After 1954, efforts to recruit workers from the Caribbean were increased because the labour shortage continued. In London and cities like London, life was expensive. Many people who lived in these cities had well-paid jobs. They did not want to do jobs that were not very well paid, such as cleaning, driving, and nursing. People from the colonies were encouraged to come to Britain to do this type of work. Between 1956 and 1958, London Transport employed 3787 Barbadians. This was still not enough and London Transport went on to recruit in Trinidad and Jamaica as well as Barbados. The National Health Service also recruited workers from British colonies. The Health Minister of the Conservative government at the time, Enoch Powell – a name you will come across again in Chapter 11 – officially welcomed West Indian nurses to Britain. By 1958, nearly 100 000 people had come from the Caribbean to settle in Britain. Many of the later arrivals were wives, parents and children of those who had come in the 1940s and early 1950s.

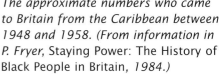

Source E

Date	Number
1948	700
1949	250
1950	200
1951	1000
1952	2000
1953	2000
1954	24000
1956	26000
1957	22000
1958	16000

The approximate numbers who came to Britain from the Caribbean between 1948 and 1958. (From information in P. Fryer, Staying Power: The History of Black People in Britain, *1984.)*

Mrs A Hart, who was a bus conductress for London Transport in 1962.

Q

7 How were Caribbean people encouraged to come to Britain during the 1950s?

How did it feel to be a *Windrush* passenger?

Arthur Curling was one of the passengers who came to Britain on *Windrush*. It was not his first visit to Britain.

At the age of sixteen, Arthur ran away from his home in Jamaica to join the RAF. He spent two years in Britain during the war and returned to Jamaica in 1946. In **Source F**, Arthur describes how his family in Jamaica thought about Britain and being British. He goes on to describe how he was unable to settle in Jamaica and why he returned to Britain on *Windrush* in 1948.

Above: *Arthur Curling in his RAF uniform during the Second World War.*
Right: *A recent photograph of Arthur Curling.*

Source F

I wouldn't say we had our own identity. We were always British. England was 'the mother country', as they used to say, and anything the English did or the British did was always right, you know. Even people like my grandmother who would listen to the radio at six o'clock every evening in the West Indies, to the World Service, and whatever was said there had to be gospel, you know... It was said by the BBC and it was from England, therefore it was right and you had to agree with it and support it. It's as simple as that...

...I went back to Jamaica in November 1946, Windrush came in 1948. I returned to England. My parents were strict. Now I had more freedom. After I reached a certain time in my life, I wanted to get away from the control of my parents.

As a matter of fact, I had a reasonably good job in Jamaica and things were looking up. It was just a matter of the island being too small. You don't realise how small until after you've travelled.

Extracts from www.bbc.co.uk/education/archive/windrush/ararthur.shtml and M. Phillips and T. Phillips, Windrush, 1998.

Q

8 Why did Arthur Curling return to Britain in 1948?

9 According to **Source D**, page 32: What type of person came on *Windrush*? Why did they come?

10 What are the differences between the reasons that Sam King, **Source D**, and Arthur Curling, **Source F**, give for coming to England?

11 As you have found out, thousands emigrated from Britain to Old Commonwealth countries, e.g. Canada and New Zealand. What suggestions can you make about why they left Britain to live in other countries?

Discuss

In **Source F** Arthur talks about Britain as the 'mother country'. This term was used by many at the time to describe the relationship between Britain and her colonies. In small groups discuss what 'mother country' might have meant in the 1940s. You could use the following questions to guide your discussion:

■ If Britain was the mother, who was the child?

■ How are mothers supposed to behave towards their children?

■ How do you think ideas about the 'mother country' were used to justify rule by Britain of the colonies?

You now have enough information to write your own answer to the question:

'Why did people come to Britain after 1945?'

The statements below are the main causes and could all be used as paragraph headings in planning your answer.

There were many refugees in Europe because of recent wars

The British colonies had fought for Britain in the Second World War

There was a labour shortage in post-war Britain

There was high unemployment and cost of living in the Caribbean

All people living in the British colonies or Commonwealth were British citizens

The British colonies in the Caribbean had a strong British identity

1 Write out each statement on separate cards or separate sheets of paper.

2 Add notes to each statement that explain them in more detail, give examples and supporting evidence.

3 Order the cards in such a way that your answer will have a clear and logical argument – each paragraph should follow on from the other.

4 You could organise your ideas about causes into different categories. All of the causes are political, economic or cultural. Read the meanings below and decide which category each cause belongs in. Use a highlighting pen or colours to identify each of the following types of cause:
- ECONOMIC: to do with money, work and industry.
- POLITICAL: to do with rights, responsibilities and citizenship.
- CULTURAL: to do with attitudes, values and feelings.

5 Which category is the most important? Why do you think this? Write down some of your reasons.

6 How could you use these ideas in your introduction or your conclusion?

7 How could you use these ideas to organise your paragraphs?

1 You could find out more about *Windrush* by using the Internet.
Do a search on 'Windrush'.
Choose the sites that are about history and / education.
Try to find a site that is written for your audience.

2 What do you want to find out from your research? Some interesting questions might be:
- How long was the journey?
- What did people do during the journey?
- Were they homesick? Were they scared? Were they excited?
- What happened when they arrived?

3 You could prepare a brief talk to give to the class about what you have found out.

4 What is the most interesting information that you have found out?

What was it like to come to Britain after the Second World War?

Many of the people who settled in Britain between 1948 and 1960 had high expectations of their new life but were soon disillusioned by the racial stereotyping and discrimination which they experienced. Racial discrimination affected all areas of their life, including finding work and accommodation.

Racial stereotype A biased and inaccurate belief about a person or group of people based on their race, colour, ethnicity, citizenship or nationality.

Racial discrimination To treat one particular group of people less favourably than others because of their race, colour or nationality (including citizenship and ethnic or national origin).

What was Britain – the 'mother country' – like in 1948?

Most of the passengers who arrived in Britain in the post-war period knew very little about the country they were coming to. Most of what they knew came from their education in the Caribbean, where Britain was portrayed as the 'mother country' – kind, caring and powerful. Many had never seen images of Britain and were surprised by the cold, the dirt, the smoke and the large number of chimneys which they associated, not with homes, but with factories. Britain seemed, in many ways, a strange and frightening country – very different to the places they had left behind.

Source A

I came from such a bright place, so much sunshine, so much colour, it was very depressing [in Britain] that time of year. They didn't know anything about us. Some people asked where you came from. Jamaica. And you could have come from the moon. They didn't know where it is and you had to tell them, it's in the Caribbean. I wished I could be back home so much it hurt, tears came into your eyes, because you missed the sort of freedom and companionship that you used to have, you know, with your own kind.

Tryphena Anderson who came to Britain in 1952 to work as a nurse. Quoted in M. Phillips and T. Phillips, Windrush, *1998.*

One of the first surprises for the new arrivals was that Britain was not as wealthy as they had expected. During the 1930s there had been terrible poverty in many parts of Britain. After 1945, Britain was slow to recover from the devastation of the Second World War. In 1948, for example, rationing was still in operation because of continuing shortages of food and other essentials. These surprises were all the more shocking because the people who came from the Caribbean knew that, as well as being citizens of the same empire, they had much in common with the British. They spoke English, shared the same national sports of cricket and football, and many were Christian in religion. Many saw themselves as 'Englishmen' and 'Englishwomen'. This sense of identity, however, was not shared by most of the white people who lived in Britain.

Even those who had already visited England during the Second World War were surprised by the reception they received from 1948 onwards. Those who had come to Britain to fight during the Second World War had, on the whole, had a warm welcome. This contrasted painfully with the reception they received on returning to Britain after the war for work purposes.

The two extracts below were both written by Jamaicans who had served in the RAF in Britain during the war. After the war they returned briefly to Jamaica and then came back to Britain on *Windrush*.

Source B

After the war finish and people see us, the first thing they're asking you, 'When are you going back to your own country?' And those are the things I didn't really like, because they say, Well, you come, you do your little bit in the war, England has won the war and now it seems as if they don't want you any more. That's how I look at it probably, I could be wrong. But I don't like that. Anyhow, the first thing, 'When are you going back to your own country?'

Cecil Holness, quoted in M. Phillips and T. Phillips, Windrush, *1998.*

A Caribbean road sweeper outside the Houses of Parliament in 1958.

Source C

The attitude of the people was changed. They were more aggressive to you. In short, they are trying to say you shouldn't be here. But there's another side. I would say a third of the people in Britain still had imperialist ideas. People from the colonies should be planting bananas and chocolate. Another third, I would say, did not really matter as long as Arsenal win on Saturday. The other third, they were just nice, ordinary people.

Sam King, quoted in M. Phillips and T. Phillips, Windrush, *1998.*

Q

1 Why do you think people from the Caribbean assumed that chimneys meant factories?

2 Use atlases, textbooks, and Internet sites to find out about the Caribbean. In what ways are the environment and culture (language, religion, and lifestyle) different to Britain?

3 In what ways were the culture of the Caribbean and Britain similar in 1948? How can you explain these similarities?

4 Use **Sources B** and **C** to explain how the attitude of some British people changed towards people from the colonies after 1945?

5 Men like Cecil Holness and Sam King were the main source of information about Britain for many in the Caribbean. How do their words help to explain why so many wanted to come to Britain after 1945?

Racism and the 'colour bar'

Finding a place to live

One of the first things that an immigrant arriving in Britain had to do was find somewhere to live. During the late 1940s and 1950s, those in need of accommodation had to have been resident for 5 years before being eligible for council housing. New arrivals were dependent, therefore, on private housing. Bombing during the war meant there was a shortage of houses as well as a shortage of labour after 1945. It was at this point that many immigrants had their first experience of the 'colour bar'.

Advertisements for vacant rooms and signs in the windows of boarding houses and newsagents, like the ones in **Source D**, often read:

Source D

Immigrants trying to find somewhere to live in London in the 1950s.

In 1956, a survey in Birmingham found that only 15 out of 1,000 white people would let a room to someone who was black. Landlords could discriminate in this way because there was no legislation to protect minorities from any kind of racism. As Lloyd Miller, who came to Britain in 1949, recollected:

Source E

So you come off [the boat]... and you go around and look... as a black man, it's very hard to get a room, you wouldn't get one. They always put on the board, 'Black –Niggers not wanted here', on the board, you know... 'No Niggers' or 'No Colour', things like that. So it's very hard to get a room.

Quoted in M. Phillips and T. Phillips, Windrush, 1998.

It was so hard to get a room that black people were forced to settle for terrible conditions and high rents in order to get shelter. Lloyd Miller eventually found a room in Islington:

Source F

That was the first room I had. And I wasn't allowed to take no visitors, I couldn't do anything. Islington, that was the first room I had. I wasn't allowed to take no visitors at all, even the couple of friends that I know... So if you want to meet up, you've got to meet around the street...

Quoted in M. Phillips and T. Phillips, Windrush, 1998.

One winter's night, when snow covered the streets, Lloyd did invite a friend into his room. The landlord called the police and Lloyd was evicted immediately.

As a result of the 'colour bar', immigrants had very little, if any, choice about where they would live or how much rent they would pay. Most were forced to settle in the 'slum' districts of London, Liverpool, Nottingham and other cities. These areas had a reputation for crime, violence, and prostitution that long preceded the arrival of the black community. The quality of housing was very poor and those who could afford to had been moving out of the inner cities to the suburbs since at least 1930. However, inner-city slums were one of the few areas where landlords would offer accommodation to those from minority ethnic groups, particularly from black minority ethnic groups. One of the most famous of these 'slum' landlords was Peter Rachman, pictured in **Source G**.

Peter Rachman owned about 100 properties in Notting Hill – large crumbling houses infested by rats and surrounded by rubbish. Before 1948, the area was populated by poor white people, many of them immigrants from Poland or Ireland. Landlords like Rachman packed as many people as possible into each living space and charged them exorbitant rents. Black people often had to pay more than double for a room compared to a white person. If a tenant complained or fell behind on payments, Rachman would send around his 'henchmen' who beat them up and destroyed their possessions. **Source H** describes the experience of living in such a building.

Experiences at work

Most of the immigrants who came from the colonies after 1948 were young men in their twenties who were trained for skilled, non-manual work. Some were professionals with qualifications in medicine and law. However, the majority ended up with lower-status jobs than their qualifications enabled them to do. They took dirty, difficult and inconvenient jobs that white people did not want, such as cleaning or jobs with night shifts. By the late 1950s, over 50% of West Indians in London had lower-status jobs than their qualifications entitled them to, because of discrimination.

Many trade unionists insisted that employers introduce a quota system for employing black people, often limiting them to 5% of the workforce. In 1955, bus workers in West Bromwich went on strike in protest against the employment of one black Asian conductor. The trade union spokesperson stated: 'I do not think there is any racial antagonism behind this'. There were similar incidents in Wolverhampton, Birmingham and Bristol. Many trade unions insisted that employers suspend the 'last in, first out' rule for redundancies by making black people redundant first. Some trade unionists used economic arguments to try to stop 'foreign' labour from coming into Britain (**Source I**).

Source G

Peter Rachman, who had also been an immigrant into Britain.

Source H

I used to live in a house, and there were nineteen children and eleven grown ups in nine rooms. It didn't have a bathroom and two families used to have to cook on the landing. One used to cook in their room and the other family I don't know how they used to do their cooking. There was one toilet.

Quoted in M. Phillips and T. Phillips, *Windrush, 1998.*

Source I

It is time a stop was put to all foreign labour entering this country. In the event of a slump occurring, the market would be flooded with cheap foreign labour... a serious deterrent to trade union bargaining power.

In 1958 this motion was put to the Trades Union Congress.

Slump/recession A period when the economy stops growing, causing unemployment and poverty.

In 1956 the current affairs television programme, *Panorama,* set out to expose the 'colour bar' at British Railways. In **Source J**, *Panorama* reporter Chris Chataway interviews a manager, Mr Davis, and a leading trade unionist, Mr Geary, at the Smithfield depot of British Railways.

Source J

CHATAWAY: now four coloured men came this morning to ask for jobs and they were turned away. Why was that? Officially the policy is that there's no colour bar.

DAVIS: Er, well, erm, there is general reluctance by the men to work with these coloured chaps...

CHATAWAY: I put much the same questions to a leading member of the Railwaymen's Union at Smithfield, Mr Geary. Now why is it that there is a prejudice here against coloured men?

GEARY: Oh there's no prejudice Mr Chataway.

CHATAWAY: Why is it that they're not taken on then?

GEARY: Well, er. It's the type of job done at a particular depot see. Speed is the question, speed. And we feel that the coloured man is apt to work at one particular pace. And, er. Also there is this much about a coloured man, the staff feel they are apt to lose their temper and resort to tactics that the average white man would not resort to.

CHATAWAY: Have you ever worked with a coloured man?

GEARY: Er, no, I haven't.

An extract from the transcript of an edition of the BBC television programme Panorama, *called 'Colour Bar', 1956.*

What was the turban ban?

Racial discrimination affected the experiences of black people at work as well as the type of jobs offered to them. In the 1950s and 1960s many Indians, in particular Sikhs from the Punjab, arrived in Birmingham in response to labour recruitment campaigns. In 1960, Birmingham City Transport enforced a turban ban on all its employees. For many Sikhs this ban was impossible to obey. Within Sikhism the turban has great religious significance because it covers the long hair which is one of the 5 Ks or principles of their religion. In response to the ban, the Sikhs at Birmingham City Transport went on strike and were finally successful in 1962 when the ban was lifted.

A Sikh man who was arrested several times for not wearing a motorcycle helmet before 1988. The Road Traffic Offenders Act (1988) included a section which allowed Sikhs to wear turbans and not helmets while riding motorcycles.

Q

6 What were the different ways in which racism could affect the experiences of black people in employment from 1948 to 1960?

7 Read **Source I**. What argument is being put forward in this motion to justify excluding people from the colonies from working in Britain? How could this argument be challenged?

8 Read **Source J**. What can we learn from this extract about racism?

9 Why was it such a problem for employees from minority ethnic groups if trade unions were racist? What was the function of trade unions?

10 One of the questions that faces any multi-ethnic society is: 'Should minorities adapt to the majority culture?' How was this question answered by Birmingham City Transport in 1960?

Consequences of discrimination

Racism and the 'colour bar' could affect black people in all areas of their life. Black people were often prevented from entering pubs or dance halls, hotels, restaurants, even hairdressers and barbers. Racial harassment and violence was also widespread.

Vince Reid was one of the few children who came to Britain from the Caribbean before 1955. He was the first black pupil at his school and describes his experiences in **Source K**. Vince eventually went to university and qualified as a teacher.

Racial discrimination and the 'colour bar' affected where black and other minority ethnic groups lived, worked and how they behaved both in the short and long term. By 1962 'black' districts or 'ghettos' had been established in most British cities. Because most black people lived in rented accommodation where they were not allowed visitors, they were forced to meet friends on the street instead. Groups of young black men on city streets were often viewed with mistrust as 'looking for trouble'. White racism made many suspicious of white people, preferring instead to mix with their own ethnic group. Much of this behaviour was misinterpreted by racists and fuelled more and more racial stereotypes which reflected badly on black people. It was a trap that was hard to escape.

How did people challenge racism?

Many black and other minority ethnic groups took positive action to counter the problems they came across. The 'Pardner system' – common in the Caribbean – was used to buy houses for black people. About five or more black people would pool their savings in order to put down a deposit on one house. Self-help groups were set up to offer advice on accommodation and employment rights. Black Christians set up their own churches and opened their own 'unofficial' clubs where calypso and blues music was played. In Bradford's Lumb Lane, an Asian sweet shop became a popular meeting place for many Asian men in the area.

In addition, not all white people were racist. It was acts of kindness by individual white people that kept many black people going when life in Britain seemed particularly bleak. For example:

Source L

If you went to sit down beside somebody on a bus, they'd shuffle up. But then somebody would look at you, see that you're as frightened as hell, and say 'Oh, mate, take no notice of them, we're not all the same.'... And just those words gave me two things: hope and comfort.

Quoted in M. Phillips and T. Phillips, Windrush, *1998.*

Source K

I was a subject of curiosity, you know, people would come up and rub your skin and see if it would rub off the black... And, of course, there was always the latent violence, you know, people want to fight you... one of the other things about the school was they didn't even give me a test to see which grade I should be put in, they just put me in the lowest grade. Then they had a sort of end-of-year examination and I moved up into the top class.

Quoted in M. Phillips and T. Phillips, Windrush, *1998.*

> **Ghetto** An area of a city with a high concentration of people from one minority ethnic group.

Activity

1 Listed below are some common racial stereotypes. Use the information in this chapter to explain how each of these stereotypes came to be believed by many people.
   - They stick together, they don't mix.
   - They live in dirty, overcrowded accommodation.
   - They hang around the streets, looking for trouble.
   - They take the jobs of white people.
   - They scrounge off the dole instead of working.
2 Which two stereotypes above contradict each other?

How has colonialism affected British culture?

Many of the racist attitudes and beliefs encountered by black people in Britain after 1945 had their origins in old ideas about slavery and Imperialism. Beliefs that white people were racially superior to black people were fostered in many ways, including children's literature, radio broadcasts, newsreels, films, novels, advertisements, and Government propaganda. By 1945, racial attitudes were an established part of British popular culture.

Imperialism A set of ideas and beliefs about empire, conquest, colonisation, and trade.

What ideas about race did Victorian people have?

The Victorian period was the height of the British Empire. In 1837, when Queen Victoria came to the throne, the British Empire was small in terms of territory and population. By 1901, when she died, it was the biggest in the world. Britain ruled over 500 million people.

The existence of the Empire made Britain one of the richest and most powerful countries in the world. Britain used her colonies to get cheap raw materials and also as a market for her own goods. The Empire was good for trade and the size of the Empire made Britain more powerful than other European countries, including having greater military power in the event of war. As the 1919 *Morning Post* newspaper stated: 'Count the Empire as one, and we need call no other nation master'.

Ideas about empire and 'race' were important in gaining and keeping control of territory. British attitudes and beliefs both about themselves and about other 'races' made colonialism and imperial rule possible. By the end of the Victorian period, British people believed that they were racially superior and often referred to other nationalities as 'lesser races'. Black people were viewed as the most inferior. These ideas went further. If British people were superior then they had the right, some said duty, to 'educate' inferior races. Racist myths were used, therefore, to justify the conquest and exploitation of other people.

The poem below uses the phrase 'white man's burden' to justify the behaviour of the colonisers, the British, towards the colonised:

'Take up the white man's burden
The savage wars of peace
Fill full the mouth of famine
And bid the sickness cease.'
Rudyard Kipling

Like many other British people, Kipling saw Britain as having a greater 'moral authority' than other countries. This meant that Britain had a duty to 'civilise' and 'improve' other people. These ideas about superiority and inferiority were supported by some scientists who 'proved' racism. Writers like Edward Long built hierarchies of 'race', largely around skin colour; whites were placed at the top of the hierarchy while blacks were put at the bottom.

How was the British Empire ruled?

The British Empire was huge and most of it was far away from Britain. It could not be ruled by force alone. Instead, small numbers of colonial administrators ruled large areas. In Africa at the end of the nineteenth century, 1,200 imperial administrators were ruling 45 million people. In Kenya, there were 117 imperial administrators ruling a population of 12 million. A belief in the superiority of the British rulers was very important, therefore, in keeping control and power in the colonies. But support for the Empire from within Britain was also crucial. Young men were needed who would be willing to work in and fight for the Empire. British people were needed to support the Empire by buying products from its colonies.

Source A

'The Rhodes Colossus Striding from Cape Town to Cairo'

This Punch cartoon from 1892 shows Cecil Rhodes straddling Africa. Rhodes was an enthusiastic supporter of empire and believed 'the more of the world that is ruled by Englishmen, the better it is for the human race.'

Q

1 Look at the cartoon, **Source A**.
   a) How is Rhodes standing in the cartoon?
   b) Where is he standing?
   c) What is the message of the cartoon about Rhodes and about Africa?

2 What is meant by 'racist myth'?
   a) What racist myths were believed about black people?
   b) What racist myths were believed about British white people?

3 How were racist myths used to justify the conquest and rule of other countries and regions?

How did ideas about the British Empire spread?

Advertising, which grew rapidly in the Victorian period, was a good way to reach as many people as possible. Victorian advertisements were designed to appeal to all social classes. They united people in their feelings of superiority compared to 'other' non-British people.

Soap adverts, for example, linked together ideas about 'cleanliness', 'whiteness' and 'superiority'. Soap, which was only used widely for the first time in the Victorian period, became a symbol of British and white 'civilisation'. Soap boxes, match boxes, biscuit tins, bottles, tea tins, chocolate bars all used images like the Pears one (**Source B**) to sell their product.

Newsreels, shown in cinemas before the film, and films were also very effective ways to promote the Empire to people. Films were the greatest source of public entertainment in Britain between the wars. In 1926 there were 3,000 cinemas in Britain, by 1940 this had risen to 5,000.

Cinema audiences saw powerful images of British rule and the Empire in some of the films they watched. Films that promoted the Empire were Rhodes of Africa (1935), Clive of India (1936), Lives of the Bengal Lancers (1934), Gunga Din (1939) and Sanders of the River (1935).

In the 1920s the Prince of Wales, son of King George V, was sent on 'imperial tours', which were filmed and shown in cinemas as newsreels. The Prince was shown being welcomed warmly wherever he went, even though many of the colonies he visited were demanding self government by this time. The purpose of the films was to promote trade within the Empire and to give an impression of unity and loyalty to people in Britain.

Source B

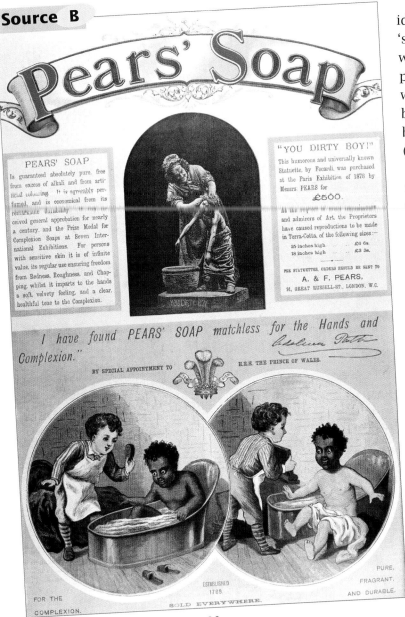

An advert for Pears' Soap in 1880.

Q

4 What is happening in the bottom half of the advert in **Source B**?

5 Why do you think the boy's head remains black while his body becomes white?

6 Why do you think the white boy is shown standing up and the black boy is shown sitting down?

The radio was another important way to inform British people about the Empire. *The Daily Mirror* newspaper said in 1924, that radio: 'brought the mother country's voice into the Australian shearing shed, the Indian plantation and the Canadian ranch-house alike'. In 1926 the Empire Marketing Board was set up to promote the Empire and trade within it. Schools were able to borrow information films like One Family (1930) which showed how the colonies enriched the lives of British people by providing them with the ingredients for their Christmas puddings, such as grapes, oranges, and raisins. Several organisations tried to publicise the value of the Empire, such as the Empire Youth Movement which grew up in the 1930s. Activities to promote the Empire included special occasions like exhibitions, lectures and concerts, as well as the sponsorship of school textbooks, maps, posters and competitions.

During the early twentieth century there was a revolution in printing and in literacy. For the first time, a wide range of magazines and comics were printed for children and teenagers. Comics like *Boys' Own Paper* 1879, *Boys of the Empire* 1900–1903, *The Boy's Friend* 1895–1927, *Gem* 1907–1939, *Magnet* 1908–1940, *Dreadnought* 1912, *Adventure* 1921, *Champion* 1922 and *Triumph* in 1924 were widely read. Popular stories in these comics usually involved a soldier-like hero who had thrilling adventures and proved his racial superiority at the same time! They all followed a formula – public school, heroes, colonial wars, sinister and dangerous foreigners, invasion scares. Villains were always foreign and international wrongs righted by 'British' boys and men.

Source C

This film from 1935 had as its hero a British Administrator in Africa called Sanders. He is presented as a firm but fair ruler. The African people are shown obeying him because he is good and 'right' while the British Empire is portrayed as a force for progress – improving the lives of African people through education and justice. In meetings between the Chiefs and the English Sanders, the Chiefs are shown sitting on the floor while Sanders is seated on a chair.

7 Use all the sources and information in this chapter to write two paragraphs about:
   a) how black people and the colonies were represented in nineteenth and early twentieth century culture;
   b) how white British people were represented in nineteenth and early twentieth century culture.

Source D

Part of the front cover of The Beano Comic, 30 July 1938.

Who was a British citizen, 1948–1968?

Between 1945 and 1968 important changes were made to who had rights of citizenship in Britain, the Empire and the Commonwealth. While everyone in Britain, the Empire and the Commonwealth had rights of British citizenship in 1948, this had been restricted by 1968. The changes happened partly because of racist attitudes towards black minority ethnic groups and partly because of changing economic needs.

Citizenship Legal rights of belonging to a particular nation or state.

Citizen A person who has rights and obligations within a particular nation or state.

El Dorado A place of great riches and opportunities

In February 1955, cinema audiences settled down to watch the following news broadcast before the main film:

Source A

In 1954, about 10,000 West Indians came to Britain. In 1955 it is believed another 15,000 will make the long journey. Already their coming has caused a national controversy, but one point must always be borne in mind: whatever our feelings we cannot deny them entry, for all are British citizens, and as such are entitled to the identical rights of any member of the Empire. Now the end of their journey is near. What will they find in the land they regard as El Dorado?

From a British Pathe Newsreel, 1955.

As the cinema news makes clear – all people living in British colonies had full rights of British citizenship in the 1950s. This meant they could hold a British passport and live and work in Britain. These rights meant they also had to fulfil all the obligations of citizenship, including payment of taxes. However, as the news item also suggests, by the late 1950s there was concern in Britain about the number of immigrants who were entering Britain from the Empire. The question: 'Who is a British citizen?' was to be answered differently in 1948, in 1962 and in 1968.

Source B

Power of the passport – more than just a travel document, the passport is also a guarantee of citizenship.

Who had British citizenship in 1948?

For many in 1948, including the Labour Government, the answer to the question 'Who is a British citizen?' was clear: all people from the colonies and Commonwealth countries should have rights of citizenship. While some felt that all these people had a moral right to citizenship, this decision was also a practical one. Britain needed the colonies and the Commonwealth for their workers because of the labour shortage. In addition, Britain was protecting its political power. By giving political

Q

1 Find the phrase in **Source A** that suggests that many British people were not happy about the arrival of immigrants from the Caribbean.

rights to the colonies and the Commonwealth, the Government was making sure that Britain would continue to get political and military support when she needed it.

The British Nationality Act (1948) said that:

All people living in Britain, British colonies and the Commonwealth have equal rights of citizenship.'

The arrival of *Windrush* in 1948 marked the start of a long debate about the question: 'Who is a British citizen?' At this time, the Empire was rapidly breaking up and more and more colonies were gaining independence and joining the Commonwealth, e.g. India in 1947. 'What rights of citizenship should these people have?' became a matter of debate within Parliament and the nation.

How and when were immigrants seen as a problem?

Minority ethnic groups suffered from racist attitudes and beliefs in Britain during the 1950s. Some minority ethnic groups were also more 'visible' than others. As a result, they may have suffered more racial discrimination, harassment and violence than other less 'visible', white minority ethnic groups, such as the Irish.

Source C

Information about Britain, immigration and labour 1945–1960

(i)   Between 1945 and 1956, 30,000 people from the Caribbean, compared to 60,000 Irish, emigrated to Britain.

(ii) From 1951 Irish emigration to Britain increased sharply due to a slump in the Irish economy. By the end of the 1960s, there were 600,000 Irish in Britain.

(iii) In the period 1945-1949, over 300,000 white immigrants emigrated to Britain from the European countries of Poland, Austria, and Italy.

(iv) In 1956 there were more unfilled vacancies than there were unemployed people in Britain. Immigrants were still needed for their labour.

Compiled from information in 'Race in the twentieth century' series and netnotes plus, Channel 4 Learning.

Source D

There was always a bit of anti-immigrant feeling, and I just think, whereas a Pole walking down Westbourne Park Road would be, you know, a white person walking down, you wouldn't know he was Polish until he opened his mouth… A West Indian or an African were very obviously from somewhere else. So I think there was some hostility towards all new immigrants and very much with West Indians.

Mervyn Jones, quoted in M. Phillips and T. Phillips, Windrush, 1998.

Q

2   'In the 1950s black people were seen as a problem out of proportion with their numbers.'

Peter Fryer, *Staying Power: The history of black people in Britain*, 1984.

Use **Sources C** and **D** and your own knowledge to say whether you agree or disagree with the historian Peter Fryer.

Racism: whose problem was it?

The Government and media tended to respond to the problem of racism as if it was a problem caused by black, not white, people. There were exceptions, such as Labour MP Tom Driberg in **Source E**.

How can there be a colour problem here? There are only 190 000 coloured people in our population of over 50 million. The real problem is not black skins but white prejudice.

Tom Driberg, Labour Party Chairperson, in a speech at the TUC Conference, 1958.

But the reaction of many people in Britain was to blame black immigration for racial problems, rather than white racist behaviour and attitudes. In addition, there were other reasons for the changing attitudes to immigrants. By 1961 economic growth in Britain had slowed down. Other European countries, such as Germany and France, had rebuilt their economies after the war and were now competing successfully with Britain. Labour was no longer in such short supply as it had been just after the war. To some people the solution to the problems of racism and recession seemed clear – limit or prevent more black people from entering Britain by passing a new law about citizenship. In 1962 a Conservative Government acted upon this 'reasoning' by passing a new law – the Immigration Act (1962).

The Immigration Act (1962) said that:

a) From now on black, including black Asian, people would have to have an employment voucher before they could enter Britain.

b) A quota was introduced on the number of vouchers available. In other words, the numbers of vouchers were limited.

c) In order to get a voucher, black people had to prove that they:
   q either already had a job offer in Britain
   q or had specialist skills
   q or had appropriate educational qualifications for Britain's needs.

d) The Act applied only to black Caribbean African and black Asian people and not to the Irish or other white minority ethnic groups and immigrants, such as Australians.

e) In 1965, the number of vouchers was further restricted to 8,500 per year.

In this way, racism became 'institutionalised' – in other words – part of the law of British society. From now on, black people within Britain, British colonies and the Commonwealth did not have the same civil rights as other people. It was the law.

Quota An official limit on the amount of something, e.g. the number of immigrants allowed by law into Britain.

Why was another Immigration Act passed in 1968?

Early in 1968 the Government began to fear a large influx of Kenyan Asians into Britain. Kenyan Asians were British Asian citizens living in Kenya, East Africa. As British citizens, they had British passports. However, Jomo Kenyatta (leader of Kenya 1963–78) had introduced an 'Africanisation' policy which looked certain to expel all foreigners, including Asians, from Kenya. Most intended to come to Britain. As racial tension increased in Britain, a Member of Parliament, Enoch Powell (see Chapters 7 and 11) made speeches around the country threatening terrible social consequences if immigration continued at a high level. The Labour Government panicked and, in just three days, a second Immigration Act was rushed through Parliament.

A family of Kenyan Asians arrive at Gatwick Airport in February 1968.

The Commonwealth Immigration Act (1968) said that:

a) Kenyan Asians with British passports were no longer allowed to enter the country.

b) A clause in the Act, however, did allow entry to white Kenyans with British passports.

Many Kenyan Asians, like the ones in **Source F**, tried to beat the ban by flying to Britain before the Act became law. They, and Asians already living in Britain, felt betrayed by their 'mother country'. As a result of the Act, about 100,000 Kenyan Asians became 'stateless' – that is – without rights of citizenship in any country.

Activity

1 On a full page, copy the table below. Depending on the size of your handwriting, you will need at least one side of A4.

2 Use the information in this chapter to complete the table. Use notes not full sentences. Examine the example already done before you start.

Name & Date of Act	Who was a citizen?	What did it say?	Why was it introduced?	Was this change or continuity?
British Nationality Act (1948)				
Immigration Act (1962)				
Commonwealth Immigration Act (1968)		■ Stopped Kenyan Asian immigration ■ Didn't stop white Kenyan immigration		

3 Use the table you have just completed to answer the following question:
   Which citizenship and immigration Act 1948–68 was a turning point?
   A 'turning point' refers to an action which dramatically changes the way things are. In other words, which Act radically changed the rights of citizenship within Britain, its Empire and the Commonwealth? To plan your answer, you should think about and write notes on the following:
   ■ Who was a British citizen?
   ■ How did citizenship and immigration legislation change British citizenship rights?
   ■ Which change was a 'turning point'?
   ■ In what ways was it a turning point? Or in what ways was it not a turning point?
   You will have to use information from the chapter to argue your case!

Discuss

Talk about the statements below. Which one is the most accurate description of Labour and Conservative policy between 1948 and 1968?
   Labour Governments were more open to immigration than Conservative Governments, 1948–1968.
   Conservative Governments were more open to immigration than Labour Governments, 1948–1968.
   Generally Labour and Conservative Governments had similar attitudes and policies to immigration, 1948–1968.

Racism and resistance in the 1960s and 1970s

During the 1960s and 1970s there was an increase both in racist incidents and racist organisations. Anti-racist organisations were formed and action was taken for civil rights. During these decades immigration became an election issue. Legislation was introduced that was intended to tackle racial discrimination.

What was the significance of the campaign in the Smethwick constituency during the 1964 general election?

Repeal Undo a law.

During the general election campaign of 1964, white prejudice against black immigrants became an important part of a local campaign in Smethwick, an industrial town in the Midlands. After the Second World War Smethwick had attracted and encouraged immigrants to work in its metal and glass industries. However, there was a shortage of housing in the town. In a population of 65,000, about 10% were black immigrants, many of whom were forced to live in overcrowded housing. In 1964, a Birmingham newspaper headline read: 'IMMIGRATION: CONTROL, CONFLAGRATION OR BETTER HOUSING?' Before the election, Labour had hinted that, if it won, it would repeal the Immigration Act (1962). In Smethwick the Labour Party had a majority of only 3,500.

Peter Griffiths, the Conservative candidate for Smethwick took as his slogan 'If you want a nigger for a neighbour, vote Labour'. He claimed a Labour victory would lead to thousands of immigrants entering Britain, whereas a Conservative victory would end immigration and protect 'British' culture and jobs. Griffiths also said that immigrants brought diseases into Britain and the presence of immigrant children held back 'British' children at school.

Griffiths' racist tactics were successful and he won his campaign in Smethwick. His victory shocked many politicians and commentators. His campaign had shown that 'playing the race card' – appealing to white racism in order to get political support – could win votes and elections.

The Smethwick election frightened political parties. It seemed to show that allowing more immigration could lose votes. This message was heard clearly by the Labour Government. Despite a Labour victory in the general election, the new Government, led by Harold Wilson, did not repeal the Immigration Act (1962). Instead, it began to draw up a white paper proposing more restrictions on immigration. In addition, a plan for a 'race relations bill' – a first attempt at a law to outlaw racism in public places, was set aside.

Source A

Also fighting in the 1964 general election was Fenner Brockway, Labour MP for Eton and Slough. Brockway was one of a minority of anti-racist politicians who spoke out specifically against the Immigration Act (1962) – see Chapter 10. While Peter Griffiths won his seat, however, Fenner Brockway lost his and was persecuted by racists.

What was 'Powellism'?

Source B

> The discrimination and deprivation, the sense of alarm and resentment lie not with the immigrant population but with those among whom they have come and are still coming. This is why to enact legislation of this kind before Parliament at the moment, is to risk throwing a match on this gunpowder... As I look ahead I am filled with foreboding. Like the Roman I seem to see the River Tiber, foaming with much blood.

Enoch Powell (pictured) had been the Conservative Minister of Health from 1960 to 1963. He had encouraged black Caribbean nurses to come to Britain to help solve the labour shortage in the National Health Service. From the mid 1960s, however, he made speeches to stop immigration. In April 1968, weeks after the Kenyan Asian crisis (see Chapter 10) and while Parliament debated a new bill against racial discrimination, Powell made what became known as his 'rivers of blood speech'. It predicted terrible consequences if immigration continued.

Powell's speeches used exaggerated, dramatic language to conjure up frightening images of the possible consequences of immigration. He appealed in a simple and direct way to some white people's prejudice, ignorance and fear. Powell was sacked from the Shadow Cabinet for making his inflammatory and racist speech. But he had supporters: on 21 April London dockers and porters marched to Parliament in support of Powell and his views. Other marches took place in the Midlands. In Slough they marched under the banner '80% of Slough people support Enoch Powell'.

In 1969 Powell's views became more extreme as he demanded the repatriation of 'coloured' immigrants already living in Britain. He continued to make speeches throughout the 1970s warning of the 'menace... of charming, wide-grinning piccaninnies' (an offensive word for black people). This racism, prevalent in the late 1960s and 1970s, became known as 'Powellism'. Powell never gained power again within government but he was important to the racist movement as an MP who openly held racist views. After Powell made his speech, there was a significant increase in racism and racist attacks on black, African Caribbean and black Asian people.

Repatriation A policy of sending people back to their 'country of origin'.

Nationalism This can either refer to the political belief that a person's country is superior to others, or to the struggle to free a country from rule or repression by another.

Patriotism Pride in and commitment to one's country.

What were the aims and methods of the National Front?

Following the success of Peter Griffiths in the Smethwick constituency in the general election of 1964, the 'National Front' (NF) was set up in 1967 when a few small fascist groups joined together. Its aim was to win political power in order to introduce racist policies and laws, particularly to end black immigration and repatriate immigrants who had settled in Britain as British citizens. The NF also campaigned against any union with Europe under the slogan 'Put British First'. The 'National Front' usually described itself as a 'nationalist' and 'patriotic'

Holocaust The mass murder of 6 million Jews by the Nazis during the Second World War.

organisation, rather than 'Nazi'. Although the NF was anti-Semitic as well as anti-immigrant, anti-black and anti-communist, most of its members tried not to be associated with the Holocaust and avoided calling themselves 'fascist'.

The NF used racist propaganda, intimidation, and violence to get across its messages. Racist propaganda blamed black people for the recession and unemployment, high prices and cuts in welfare of the mid-to-late 1970s. Newspapers and posters were distributed and black people were intimidated on the street. In particular, the NF aimed to provoke the black community by organising racist marches and rallies in housing areas with a high density of black people. In 1974, a National Front rally led to the death of a white anti-racist demonstrator called Kevin Gately.

Why did support for the NF rise and fall in the 1960s and 1970s?

When the National Front was set up in 1967, it had only 1500 members. However, when Powell was sacked from the Shadow Cabinet in April 1968, support for the NF increased as some Conservatives left their own party in disgust and joined the NF. During the 1970s, following the Immigration Act (1971) – see page 55, support for the NF increased again. The majority of its active support was from young, white working-class men, many of whom became 'skinheads'. The NF had no national political success but a few local successes. It polled 10,000 votes in the Leicester local elections of 1973. In 1976, two members of the NF were elected as local councillors in Blackburn. In 1977 a National Front candidate won 16.2% of the vote in a by-election in West Bromwich.

In 1978, the Conservative Party leader, Margaret Thatcher, said on the BBC TV programme *Panorama* that there were many British people who were afraid that they might be 'swamped by people with a different culture'. She said that to ignore this issue of immigration would drive even more people to join the NF and added 'we are not in politics to ignore people's worries but to deal with them'. As a result, she won back much of the Conservative support lost to the National Front. When Mrs Thatcher made these comments, black people made up less than 4% of the British population. In 1979 the Conservative Party won the general election and support for the NF declined sharply and never recovered. In addition, its members increasingly disagreed with each other, destroying any unity. In 1982 a new party, the British National Party emerged from the disagreements in the NF ranks. In September 1993 the BNP won a local council seat in East London. In the 2001 general election, the BNP won 16.4% of the votes in Oldham, compared with 17.7% for the Conservatives and 51.6% for Labour. It was the BNP's best ever election result.

Source C

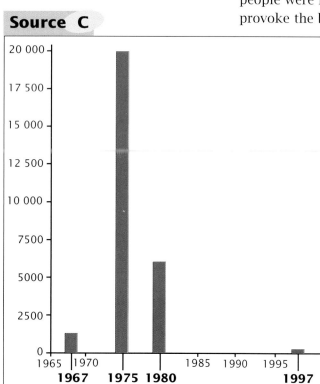

The rise and fall of the National Front.

Q

1 Explain how the 'race card' was played in Smethwick?

2 Why do you think that many members of the National Front tried to distance themselves from Nazism?

3 Why did the NF stress that they were 'patriotic' and 'nationalist' rather than 'fascist'?

How did black and white people resist and challenge racism?

As racism increased in the 1960s and 1970s, so did support for anti-racist organisations from black and white people. Socialist organisations, in particular, played an important part in supporting anti-racist movements. The day after Powell's 'rivers of blood' speech, on 21 April 1968, the Black People's Alliance (BPA) was formed, in the Midlands. During the 1970s anti-racist organisations and black organisations increased in number, offering support to minority ethnic groups at a local level and campaigning against racism at a national level. The Immigration Act (1971) attracted the largest anti-racist, anti-fascist demonstration ever. Anti-racist organisations also organised 'counter marches' to prevent the NF from spreading their racism and intimidating people on the streets and at home.

What was the battle of Lewisham 1977?

In August 1977, the National Front announced that it was going to march through the mainly black area of Lewisham in south London. A massive demonstration of local people and national anti-racist and socialist groups tried to stop the march. As in the battle of Cable Street (pages 26–27), the police allowed racists and fascists to march while arresting anti-racists – a number of whom were seriously injured. Despite this, the anti-racists were successful and the NF could not continue. This was a serious defeat for the NF and gave greater confidence to anti-racists. Immediately following the 'battle' – the Anti-Nazi League (ANL) was formed and the Rock against Racism campaign was launched to use music to fight racism.

The Anti-Nazi League aimed to expose NF members and supporters as 'Nazis' not 'patriots', to organise themselves to resist racism and to resist racist marches and rallies in particular. Martin Webster of the NF said in 1981: 'The sheer presence of the ANL had made it impossible to get NF members on the streets, had dashed recruitment and cut away at their [NF] vote.'

Source D

Another possible reason for the decline of the National Front was the success of anti-racist organisations. This is an anti-BNP demonstation in London in 1993.

Q

4 Make a sketch of **Source C**. Use the information in this chapter so far to explain each increase and decrease in membership of the National Front.

5 One popular slogan of the anti-racist movement was: 'The National Front is a Nazi Front'. Why do you think they stressed the connection with Nazism while many in the NF did not?

How did the Government respond to racism and anti-racism in the 1960s and 1970s?

In 1965 the first Race Relations Act was passed and, in 1976, a second Act was passed.

THE RACE RELATIONS ACT (1965)	
Strengths	**Weaknesses**
■ The Act made racism in public places illegal. ■ It made 'incitement to racial hatred' an offence.	■ It ignored racism in housing and employment, the two areas where racial discrimination caused the most problems and disadvantage for minority ethnic groups. ■ No single body of people had powers of enforcement of the Act. ■ Nobody was made to feel responsible for making sure that the Act worked or was known about.

Results

■ The Act was very limited.

■ In practice the 'incitement to racial hatred' was used to charge more blacks than whites.

■ The Act was not effective against racism – racism did not decline and racists were generally not punished by the law.

THE RACE RELATIONS ACT (1976)	
Strengths	**Weaknesses**
■ This Act made racial discrimination unlawful in employment, housing, and education. ■ Following the passage of the Act, the Commission for Racial Equality was set up to make sure that people knew about the Act and obeyed it.	■ Resources, such as money, were needed for victims of racism to take legal action to prosecute offenders. ■ Racism was hard 'to prove'. No data had ever been collected on how many blacks and whites applied for jobs, were successful, employed, promoted, well paid and so on. As a result it was hard to show clearly whether racial discrimination had happened or not.

Results

After the death of Stephen Lawrence (see Chapter 14) the Act was widely criticised for failing to make public bodies, including the police, take positive action against racism.

Q

6 How did the Race Relations Act (1976) improve on the Race Relations Act (1965)?

7 Why was it difficult to make the Race Relations Acts effective against racism?

8 In 1991, the national Census asked about ethnic origin for the first time. Why do you think it was seen as important to collect data about ethnic origin?

9 The Census also records occupation, address, size of family, income. How could this information be used to find out about racial discrimination?

Immigration law in the 1960s and 1970s

Perhaps the biggest problem in making the Race Relations Acts effective against racism, was the wider background in which they had to work. At the same time that legislation was introduced against racism, immigration laws were operating that discriminated between black and white people. In Chapter 10 you found out about the Immigration Act (1962), which restricted black immigration for the first time, and the Commonwealth Immigration Act (1968), a rushed attempt to stop Kenyan Asians who had British passports coming to Britain.

The Immigration Act (1971) made immigration by black people from the Commonwealth into Britain even more difficult. The Act distinguished between patrials and non-patrials. While patrials could enter freely, live and work in Britain, non-patrials could not. Patrials were almost all white, many coming from the 'Old' Commonwealth countries of Australia and New Zealand. The discrimination of the Act was very controversial and hotly debated in Parliament before it became law. In 1973, Britain joined the EEC (European Economic Community) – the citizens of which were able to enter and work in Britain freely.

Patrials People born in Britain or with a parent or ancestor born in Britain.

Non-patrials People not born in Britain or without a parent or ancestor born in Britain.

Rese...

1 Find out more about Equiano and Duleep Singh. Use their names and key words from the captions to research the Internet, library catalogues and book indexes.

2 Equiano and Duleep Singh were part of a long tradition of black political activism. Find out about the following black political activists:

a) In Britain
Krishna Menon
Dusé Mohamed Ali
Surinder Bassi
Shapurji Saklatvala
Claudia Jones
Bernie Grant
Diane Abbot
A. Siranandan

b) In other countries
Martin Luther King
Malcolm X
Mahatma Gandhi
Marcus Garvey
Nelson Mandela
Steve Biko
Walter Rodney
W.E.B. Du Bois
Rosa Parkes
Frantz Fanon

Olaudah Equiano, who campaigned against the slave trade in the eighteenth century. He published a best-selling autobiography in 1789.

Sophia Duleep Singh, daughter of the Maharajah Duleep Singh, selling the Suffragette *in 1913. She was active in the suffragette movement.*

What was happening to race relations and civil rights in the rest of the world?

Source E

Source F

A civil rights march in Londonderry in Northern Ireland in 1968. On 30 January 1972, British troops opened fire on another civil rights march through Londonderry. Fourteen men, all unarmed, were killed. The legal investigation into these killings continues today and, as yet, nobody has been convicted. The march was for 'civil rights' – including the right of the Catholic minority to be treated equally and fairly. Many Catholics were discriminated against in housing and employment in Northern Ireland.

In the post-war period and up to the 1970s, many colonies gained independence from Britain and joined the 'New' Commonwealth. These newly independent countries were often held back by the economic and political effects of imperialism, e.g. economic underdevelopment and inexperience of self-rule and democratic processes, such as voting. This is the Kenyan independence ceremony in December 1963. The Kenyan leader, Jomo Kenyatta (see page 48) is in the centre of the photograph.

Source G

In 1959 the anti-apartheid movement was started as a response to the brutal and racist regime in South Africa known as 'apartheid'. The movement used lobbies, demonstrations and boycotts of South African products to demand the release of Nelson Mandela from prison and to put pressure on world governments to act against apartheid. This is a demonstration in Britain in 1985.

Source H

In the 1960s and 1970s the Rastafarianism movement grew in Britain, attracting black and white people to its culture and particularly to its music. Rastafarianism looked to Africa, particularly Ethiopia, as the 'spiritual' homeland of African Caribbean people – a place where they could be proud of their heritage and live equally. The lyrics and rhythms of songwriter Bob Marley from Jamaica (pictured), e.g. lyrics like 'Get up, stand up, Stand up for your rights', inspired anti-racist movements and beliefs.

Source I

In the 1960s, the 'Black Power' movement grew in the USA. This was a militant movement, which demanded radical solutions to racial discrimination and encouraged black people to defend themselves against white aggression. Pictured are two black American athletes giving the Black Power salute at the Olympic Games in Mexico in 1968.

In what ways are **Sources E–I** relevant to understanding race relations in Britain in the 1960s and 1970s?

Racism and anti-racism in the 1960s and 1970s: making links and connections

1 Draw 8 columns and 5 rows onto a very large sheet of paper, for example, A3 size. Label them as shown.

Period	Racist movement	Anti-racist movement	Government anti-racist legislation	Government immigration legislation	Economic trends	Other significant dates, e.g. general elections	Global trends & events
1960–1965			Race Relations Act (1965) said...	Immigration Act (1962) said...	Economic boom of 1950s starts to slow down.	1964 and 1966 general elections, with Labour victories in both.	
1966–1970	NF set up 1967. Aims... Methods...	BPA set up 1968.		1968 emergency Commonwealth Immigration Act to stop Kenyan Asians entering Britain.		1970 general election, Conservative victory.	
1971–1975					Recession from 1973 onwards.	1974 general election, with Labour victory.	
1976–1980	NF support declines rapidly after 1979.	1977 battle of Lewisham.			Unemployment was high for all and black people suffered the most.	1979 general election, ...victory.	

Racist 'apartheid' rule in South Africa

Colonies gain independence from Britain

Anti-apartheid movement

Civil Rights Movement grows, e.g. Ireland and USA

Rise in support for NF

Black power movement grows

Smethwick election campaign

Britain joins EEC

---

2 Use what you have learnt in this chapter to fill in the table.
Some examples have been, or partly been, done for you.
Read the examples then add the other statements on this spread.
Use the chapter to decide where to put each one.

3 What connections can you find between pieces of information?
How might economic factors help to explain political events?
Jot down any interesting links and ideas about links that you may have.

4 Study the columns on Government legislation and dates of general
elections. Does the information in your table support the view below
of the Labour Government 1964–1970?

'The government's strategy under Harold Wilson was to limit
immigration but to condemn racial discrimination.'

Butler and Jones, Britain in the Twentieth Century.

5 What evidence is there in this chapter that supports or disagrees with
Richard Crossman's beliefs below about immigration and votes?

'Ever since the Smethwick election it has been quite clear that
immigration can be the greatest potential vote-loser for the Labour
Party if we are seen to be permitting a flood of immigrants to come
and blight the central areas in all our cities.'

Richard Crossman, Diaries of a Cabinet Minister, 1975.

Bob Marley and rastafarianism very popular

ANL set up

Immigration Act (1971)

Powellism

Race Relations Act (1976)

The Brixton riot of 1981: trends, tensions, and triggers

In 1981 there were violent disturbances in Brixton that became known as the Brixton riot. There were further riots in over 30 towns and cities across Britain. A Government Inquiry investigated the causes of the riots and made recommendations to prevent future trouble. In 1985 and in 2001, however, there were more riots in many British cities. The causes of the riots have been interpreted differently by groups and individuals.

Source A

Left: A wrecked car at the Toxteth boundary, Liverpool in July 1981, following the riots. Above: Firemen damp down the burnt out shells of buildings in Lodge Lane Toxteth following a night of rioting.

What happened in April 1981?

In April 1981 a riot broke out in Brixton. In the space of a few days, at least 7000 police and about 5000 young people, both black and white, clashed in the streets. Cars, shops, pubs and houses were damaged or destroyed, and bricks and petrol bombs were thrown. As the situation in Brixton began to calm down, the rioting spread to other areas, especially inner cities with black minority ethnic communities. Over 30 towns and cities experienced violence and disruption in 1981 (**Source A**). Millions of pounds' worth of damage was caused, civilians and police were injured and CS gas (tear gas) was used against crowds of black and white young people.

Riots were not a new phenomenon to British life. There had been frequent riots in the eighteenth and nineteenth centuries and in the periods before and after the First World War. However, these were the first riots involving clashes of large numbers of black people against the police. As Britain began the process of repairing the damage, people asked themselves: 'What has gone wrong? How can future disturbances be prevented?'

Where in Britain did minority ethnic groups settle after 1948?

Most of the passengers who came to Britain on *Windrush* in 1948 were sent to stay in a disused air-raid shelter in Clapham until they were able to find permanent accommodation. Most eventually settled in nearby Brixton, in the Borough of Lambeth, because it had cheap houses for rent and a labour exchange office on Coldharbour Lane. This settlement of immigrants from the Caribbean changed the character and atmosphere of the area, enriching it in new and unique ways. Brixton market sold food and other goods from the Caribbean and Africa; African Caribbean cafes, clubs and newspapers, such as the *West Indian Gazette*, were established. As a result, many other black African Caribbean immigrants who arrived in the 1950s and 1960s also settled in Brixton. By 2000, 30% of the population of Lambeth were from minority ethnic groups.

The pattern of settlement in Lambeth was similar to that of other parts of Britain after 1948. Most people from minority ethnic groups settled in the same area where other members of their community had already settled. As a result, different towns, cities and areas of cities became the centre of communities from particular minority ethnic groups. For example, Southall in London became a focus for the Asian community, particularly Punjabis. Many immigrants from Pakistan, Bangladesh and India settled in Bradford after 1948, while the East End of London also attracted Asians as well as African Caribbeans.

Towns and cities with large communities from different minority ethnic groups.

1 Find out about the different communities which have settled in your own area, or in an area which particularly interests you. Try to find out their reasons for settling in the area. How long have the different communities been there? Can you identify patterns of settlement over time?

2 Cardiff, Glasgow, Bristol, London and Liverpool have the longest settled black communities, many coming from Africa and Asia from 1600 onwards. Study the map to suggest why these five cities have the longest-settled black communities.

Why did the Brixton riot happen in April 1981?

Long before 1981 the black community of Brixton had a history of poor relations with the police. The vast majority of police officers were white and were viewed increasingly by many black people as racist and hostile. One major source of tension was the use of the 'sus' law in inner-city areas. The **'sus'** law – officially Section 4 of the Vagrancy Act which had been passed in 1824 – was used in the 1950s, 1960s and 1970s to arrest young black men without evidence of a crime. The law allowed two police officers to arrest someone for 'acting **sus**piciously'. No crime was necessary for the arrest. The police officers only needed to witness 'suspicious' behaviour on two occasions by the same person - even if the two occasions were just minutes apart! The law was widely abused. Black people campaigned against it and the law was repealed in the 1970s. However, removing the law did not prevent racist harassment of black people by the police. Black men had a much higher chance of being stopped, searched, and arrested than white males. In 1979 a report by Lambeth Council described the police presence in Brixton as being like 'an army of occupation'.

In addition, black people suffered from racist discrimination in other important areas of their lives, such as employment and housing. From the late 1950s onwards, unemployment and poverty was highest amongst minority ethnic groups.

What was SWAMP '81?

On Monday 6 April 1981 a new police operation began in London called SWAMP '81. The aim was to prevent crime by stopping and searching as many people as possible in a one-week period. 112 police officers in 10 squads were involved in SWAMP and 4 of those 10 squads were sent to Brixton. The police involved were given the following instructions:

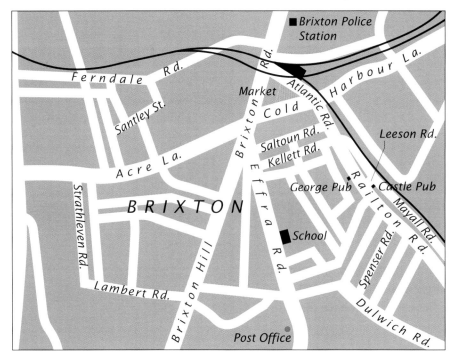

'The purpose of this operation is to flood identified areas on 'L' District to detect and arrest burglars and robbers. The essence of the exercise is, therefore, to ensure that all officers remain on the streets and success will depend on a concentrated effort of 'stops', based on powers of surveillance and suspicion.'

While 943 'stops' were made in Brixton during the week of Monday 6 April to Friday 10 April, there was only one arrest for robbery. The presence of a large number of police, targeting black people rather than white, however, caused extra resentment and anger on the streets of Brixton.

Flashpoint Brixton

Friday 10 April:

On the fifth day of Swamp '81, as one eyewitness said, Brixton erupted into a 'fireball of anger'. In the afternoon, a police patrol stopped on Railton Road to help a black youth who had been stabbed. An ambulance was called but as police were bandaging the youth in their car, it was attacked by a group of young black men who thought the police were trying to take someone way. Fighting broke out between police and the crowd of youths and lasted about three quarters of an hour. Bottles were thrown through the police vehicles' windscreens. This particular incident ended when police reinforcements arrived, but the build up of police patrols in the area carried on through the rest of the night and into Saturday. A white female eyewitness who lived in Spenser Road said that when she came home on Friday evening at 6pm, Dulwich Road was filled with 'police and sirens and vehicles. There were so many I thought they were on some sort of exercise'.

Saturday 11 April:

Police decided to carry on with Operation Swamp. A black female eyewitness living on Railton Road told a reporter: 'At 9am on Saturday morning, I thought there must be some trouble today because the police were in twos all the way down Railton Road, Atlantic Road and Coldharbour Lane'. All afternoon, groups of young people gathered on the streets.

4.45pm

A crowd gathered to watch a taxi driver being searched. The police found nothing but the young man, after fighting with one officer, was taken away in a van. Missiles were thrown at the van by youths, breaking some of its windows. The police called for reinforcements. Up to 60 police vans arrived and tried to disperse the crowd but the fighting got worse.

5pm

An abandoned police car was set on fire in Atlantic Road. Shops were broken. The fighting spread into Railton Road and Mayall Road. Police started to use their riot shields and to form cordons at the end of Railton Road.

6.30pm

The first petrol bombs were thrown by black and white youths. They set fire to cars in Railton and Leeson Roads. The fire brigade was sent for but could not reach Railton Road. Later a fire brigade officer said that 'we were not able to get beyond Saltoun Road and we then began to get reports of other fires we couldn't attend to. Every time we tried to attend to a fire, we were attacked. We've never had this sort of disturbance before'.

7.40pm

Youths commandeered a fire engine that they drove up and down Railton Road. A petrol bomb set fire to the Windsor Castle pub on Leeson Road and the George pub in Railton Road. A white family living in Railton Road had their door

A line of police with riot shields looks down Railton Road at cars set on fire by rioters.

kicked in by a group of eight black youths who threatened them with knives and demanded money. A black family tried to stop the youths but failed.

A crowd throwing missiles pushed police down Railton Road towards Atlantic Road. Police grouped in Mayall Road to try to push the rioters back. Buildings were burnt, including the post office and school on Effra Road. Serious looting of shops began.

9.30pm

Electricity failed on Mayall Road and the Windsor Castle pub collapsed, destroyed by fire.

10pm

Police began to regain control of the area.

Throughout the night, 14 properties were destroyed or damaged by fire and 22 vehicles, including police cars and fire engines, were burnt out. The violence continued over the weekend. About 7,000+ police were on streets and, according to estimates reported in the *Guardian* newspaper, about 5,000 rioters.

Source for information about the Brixton riot: the Guardian *newspaper.*

What happened after the Brixton riot of 1981?

The riots of 1981 were so destructive and widespread that the Conservative Government felt it had to act very quickly to prevent more riots from happening. The government appointed Lord Scarman to find out about the causes of the Brixton riot, especially to find out about the problems of policing the inner cities. In order to investigate why the riot happened, Scarman interviewed many people including police, local community organisations, local councillors, black organisations and academics. In his Report, Scarman reached the following conclusions:

n The riot was not caused by the behaviour of the police.

n The police were not, on the whole, racist although there was 'occasional racial prejudice'.

n Black people in Brixton suffered from racial discrimination and from rising unemployment and these were also causes of the riot.

Scarman also made some recommendations for the future. He said that positive action was needed to stop racism. He also said that the police should be more locally based and liaise with local community organisations. But in 1985 there were further riots in Handsworth in Birmingham, Broadwater Farm in Tottenham, Moss Side in Manchester and Toxteth in Liverpool. In Tottenham, in London, a police officer was stabbed to death. For many, the riots of 1985 were a sign of the failure of governments to solve the problems of racism and of poverty, especially in the inner cities.

How have the riots been portrayed?

Below are two different views of the causes of the riots of the 1980s.

Source C

On the Haringey Against Racism Festival march from Broadwater Farm in July 1986.

Source D

This is not a racial issue as such. It is exclusively a crowd of black hooligans intent on making life unbearable and indulging in criminal activities.

Kenneth Oxford, Chief Constable of Merseyside, speaking about the Toxteth riots of 1985.

Source E

The way to prevent future riots, it said, was to rid the police force of racism – nothing else would do.

The view of the Brixton Defence Campaign, as described by 'Homebeats' CD.Rom, Institute of Race Relations, 1997.

A fire crew on the streets of Oldham in May 2001, as gangs of youths hurl petrol bombs at police officers and put up burning barricades during the second night of racial disturbances in the town. In 2001 riots and racial disturbances also took place in Burnley, Bradford, Leeds and Aylesbury. A wide range of causes was suggested after the riots, including: poverty, racism, poor housing, unemployment levels, BNP activism and terrorism, police behaviour and attitudes, and segregated schooling.

Q

1   In what ways are **Sources D** and **E** different?

2   Which description of the causes of the riots is the most accurate? Why do you think this?

3   Write a short essay that answers the big question:
   'What were the causes of the Brixton riot?'
   Read the chapter again and write a paragraph about each of the following things.
   Introduction: Why was the Brixton riot important?
   Trends: In what ways were British life and society changing?
      For example, black minority ethnic groups were settled mainly in the inner cities, where there was poverty and rising unemployment.
   Tensions: What were the long-standing problems between different people, communities and institutions, such as the police force.
      For example, the 'sus' law was used to arrest black people up until its repeal in the 1970s.
   Triggers: What made the Brixton riot start in April 1981 and not earlier or later?
   Conclusions: Do your conclusions agree with those of the Scarman Report?

Why did people come to Britain in the late twentieth century?

Since the Second World War the pattern of migration into and out of Britain has changed. This has been due to changes in the law, wars, abuses of human rights, poverty, famine, and the formation of the European Union. Since 1990 the rights of refugees and asylum seekers in Britain have also changed and become a controversial political issue.

Source A

Displaced persons in Bosnia in 1995. Most refugees and displaced persons arrive with no money and few possessions. Many have been tortured, imprisoned, and persecuted, or have witnessed traumatic events such as war and genocide (the mass extermination of a particular people). The way that a refugee is treated, therefore, is crucial to their survival and recovery, both physically and mentally.

Refugee A person who leaves their own country because they face persecution because of their race, religion, political beliefs, nationality or membership of a particular social group.

British national A citizen of an ex British colony. Lost right to British citizenship in the British Nationality Act (1981).

Displaced person A refugee who leaves their home but not their country.

Sanctuary/asylum A place of safety.

Who came to Britain in the late twentieth century?

Towards the end of the twentieth century, migration and settlement patterns changed across the world, including Britain. There was less immigration into Britain of those with British citizenship who had been born in the colonies or the Commonwealth than there had been in the 1950s. The immigration laws of the 1960s and 1970s and the British Nationality Act (1981) made it difficult for a British national to enter Britain freely. Instead, in the 1980s and 1990s, it was citizens of the European Union who were able to enter Britain freely. Work permits did continue to be issued but to American and Japanese business people rather than to workers from the Caribbean.

The British Nationality Act (1981) said that:
a British citizen was either someone born to British parents or born abroad to British parents. British nationals were no longer British citizens. This act changed the definition of who was a British citizen.

Another important feature of population movement in the late twentieth century was the growing number of refugees across the world. In the late 1990s there were over 20 million refugees in the world and around 30 million displaced persons. Most of these refugees were living in the poorer continents of Africa and Asia and only about 5% found sanctuary in Europe. In 2000 the highest number of applications for asylum in Europe came from the former Yugoslavia, Iraq, Afghanistan, and Iran.

Throughout history people have had to leave their homes and find refuge elsewhere. As you found out in Chapter 1, many different ethnic groups have come to Britain over time in need of sanctuary. Many have settled permanently, becoming a vital part of British society and culture. Over time, people have also left Britain in search of refuge, including Jewish people during the persecution of the Middle Ages and Irish nationalists from Northern Ireland during the twentieth century.

However, in the late twentieth century, there have been important changes in the number of refugees, where they come from and their destinations, their reasons for leaving home, their human rights and how they are treated. In recent years, many countries in Western Europe, including Germany, France and Britain, have changed their laws on asylum. These changes have made it harder for refugees to apply for asylum in these countries and have changed the rights which they have as asylum seekers living in another country.

Source B is the story of Zuhra Bahman, a 17 year old who fled the very brutal and repressive Afghan government. About 6,000 refugees under the age of 17 claim asylum in the UK every year. Nearly 1000 come on their own, without a family member. On arrival they are placed in local authority care.

Source B

"*I was sitting in my room listening to the bullets hitting my roof like raindrops; rape, death, injuries and blood were all I was thinking about. I was not sure what might happen next, I wasn't sure if I would ever see my friends and relatives again. Maybe someone is dead or maybe I'll die before seeing them. I was thinking about my future, which seemed dark.... I wanted to shout to ask for my rights and to stop the war but I couldn't. I was too weak. Then I decided to leave my country, family and friends, language and culture and seek asylum in the UK. When I came to the UK I realised that I am not the only one who has suffered at a young age. There were many others as young or even younger than me, who had gone through much more terrible suffering than I had.*"

Zuhra Bahman from Afghanistan, quoted on the web site of The Refugee Council at www.refugeecouncil.org.uk.

What rights do asylum seekers and refugees have in Britain?

Immigration and Asylum Acts were passed in 1993, 1996 and 1999. These laws changed life for asylum seekers in Britain. They no longer have rights to benefits and are no longer allowed to work. Instead, they must rely on charity and local authority care for housing and food. This has meant that asylum seekers in some parts of Britain are better treated than in other parts. A system of 'dispersal' has meant that some have been sent to areas of Britain not used to looking after asylum seekers. Instead of benefits, adult asylum seekers receive £36 worth of vouchers a week, only £10 of which can be exchanged for cash. There have been many problems with the vouchers. Many asylum seekers have had to wait weeks for their vouchers, relying on charity or begging in order to survive. Vouchers are only issued for specific supermarkets and have to be spent in one go. Vouchers also mark out asylum seekers as different to others on benefits.

Asylum seekers who use false documents to flee their own country can be prosecuted on arrival in Britain. This is despite the fact that many have to use false documents in order to escape. Since 1999 it has been possible to deport asylum seekers before their claim is dealt with and it has become harder to appeal when a claim for asylum had been refused. Some asylum seekers have been sent to detention centres and prisons on arrival. In 2000, about 1,000 asylum seekers were being detained without charge, trial or time limit. In addition, it has become harder for refugees to reach Britain in the first place. Those who transport asylum seekers without proper travel documents can be fined £2000. Sometimes refugees travel through many countries to reach a country that will accept them. They have to do this because different countries have different lists of what is a 'safe' country of origin. Algerians, for example, are more likely to be seen as genuine refugees in Britain than they are in France. France is more likely to say that Algeria is a 'safe' country.

What is 'trafficking' in people?

Because it has become harder to come to Britain to claim asylum, many refugees, in desperation, smuggle themselves in. As a result, 'trafficking' – the smuggling of illegal immigrants across borders into and around Europe – has become a profitable business for criminals. Thousands have died during dangerous journeys across sea and land. At the end of the journey, many are then forced into prostitution or sweated labour to pay back the 'traffickers' who smuggled them, or because they are unable to claim any benefits to live on or to find work legally.

Refugees and Human Rights

1 Use web sites, including The Refugee Council, Amnesty International and The Home Office, to find out about the rights and treatment of refugees in Britain and other countries today.

2 What are the differences and similarities between the rights of refugees in other countries and in Britain?

3 Discuss how the following might affect the rights and experiences of refugees in Britain:
- Dispersal
- Vouchers
- Benefits and Housing
- Detention

4 Refugees in late twentieth century Britain were more highly qualified and included a higher proportion of professional people than the general British population. What might be the cost to Britain of not allowing them to work?

What attitudes do people in Britain have towards refugees?

The rights and treatment of refugees in Britain have been very controversial. British people disagree about how refugees should be treated. Some have claimed that Britain is a 'soft touch' for refugees, being too generous with benefits and encouraging 'bogus' applications. Others have criticised Britain for its racist and intolerant attitudes to refugees. Nick Hardwick in **Source C**, blamed some newspapers for not telling the whole truth about refugees and using emotional language to feed prejudice. Words and phrases such as 'flooded', 'swamped', 'scroungers', 'tidal wave', 'cheats' have been used often in articles and headlines about refugees such as **Source D**.

The extract below is from a survey carried out into the attitudes of readers of *Reader's Digest* magazine in July 2000.

Source C

Public 'misinformed' on refugees

- 63% thought too much was done to assist asylum seekers in Britain.
- The average respondent assumed refugees were given £113 a week to live on. In fact a single adult receives £36.
- On Britain's racial mix – the average person thought 26% of the population is from a minority ethnic group but the true figure is 7%.

'Worrying implications'

Eight out of 10 believe refugees come to Britain because they regard it as 'a soft touch' and two-thirds (66%) thought there were too many immigrants.

'Not surprising'

Nick Hardwick, chief executive of The Refugee Council, said: 'This is depressing reading but not surprising. The public are hostile and fed on a constant diet of prejudice.' He added, 'The public are badly misinformed. The truth is that refugees are fleeing life-threatening situations, that last year 54% of initial asylum decisions were positive, that asylum seekers are given the bare minimum on which to survive.'

From bbc.co.uk/hi/english/uk/newsid_986000/986295.stm Monday, 23 October, 2000

1 Read **Source C**. How does the survey support Nick Hardwick's view that the British people are misinformed about refugees and immigrants?

2 Why do you think it is important to be informed about refugees and immigrants?

3 Read **Source D**. How does it use language to arouse emotion and prejudice about refugees?

4 Write a letter to the journalist in **Source D** challenging his view of refugees. Use information from this chapter to support your own point of view.

Find up to 5 articles from different newspapers about refugees.
What attitudes are shown in:
- Choice of headline
- Language, for example, use of adjectives to describe asylum seekers
- Facts reported, for example, what information is given and not given about reasons why a particular group of people would want to flee their country
- Images used, for example, cartoons, photographs, maps
- Other?

Source D

We resent the scroungers, beggars and crooks who are prepared to cross every country in Europe to reach our generous benefits system.

From The Sun, 7 March 2001

Discuss the following statements about refugees and asylum seekers. For each statement, use information that you have learnt in this book and in your own research to say whether you agree or disagree. You could plan a debate on the issue, inviting local community representatives as well as other members of your school.

- 'Refugees are scapegoats. They get the blame for social problems in Britain, e.g. housing shortages, drugs, crime.'
- 'Britain cannot afford not to take refugees. Their skills are needed and they can make a positive contribution to British life.'
- 'Britain is one of the most popular destinations for refugees in Europe because it is so generous.'
- 'We should offer sanctuary because one day we may need sanctuary ourselves.'
- 'Britain, like all countries, has a moral obligation to protect human rights.'
- 'Britain cannot afford more refugees. They must go somewhere else.'

Why do refugees flee their own countries?

Roma gypsies and travellers
Roma gypsies and travellers have had to flee many countries in Europe, including Bosnia, Slovakia, Kosovo, and the Czech Republic, because of persecution against them and abuses of their human rights. Many have fled to western European countries but have also faced persecution in those countries. There is evidence that Roma asylum seekers are not getting fair and equal treatment with other asylum seekers in many western European countries.

Czech Rep.
Slovakia
Romania
Chechnya
Bosnia
Italy
Georgia
Kosovo
Armenia
Azerbaijan
Albania
Turkey
Spain
Gibraltar
Morocco
Iraq
Iran

Kosovo
Since the early 1990s, large numbers of ethnic Albanians from Kosovo, part of the Federal Republic of Yugoslavia, have been seeking sanctuary in the UK as well as other European countries. They have been fleeing persecution from the Yugoslav government. There has been evidence of massacres of civilians since the 1990s and, in the late 1990s, around 850,000 Kosovan Albanians fled ethnic cleansing by Serb forces.

Kurdish people
Kurdish people do not have their own state or country. The area they have always lived in now forms part of Turkey, Iran and Iraq. They have been persecuted in these countries for most of the twentieth century. In 2000 there were nearly half a million Kurdish refugees in Europe and the Middle East.

Iraq
There have been reports of human rights abuses, including against the Kurdish minority, under the leadership of Saddam Hussein, President of Iraq since 1979. A popular uprising against Hussein in 1991 was brutally suppressed, causing widespread loss of life and devastation. All other opposition to the Government has also been crushed.

Trafficking
Every year millions of Africans flee wars, persecution, and poverty. Some make their way across the desert to Morocco and then try to cross the nine-mile-wide Gibraltar Straits into southern Spain. It is a terrible journey and many drown when their boats or rafts sink. About 3,000 died trying to cross between 1998 and 2001. In 1997, at least 170 people drowned attempting to cross the Adriatic from Albania to Italy. In 1998, 90 Romanian immigrants nearly suffocated inside a lorry in Italy. In June 2000, 58 Chinese illegal immigrants were found suffocated inside a lorry at Dover.

Sudan
War and abuses of human rights in Sudan have caused many to leave their homes and seek sanctuary in Europe and other African countries.

Sudan
Somalia

Rwanda
In 1994 about 1.5 million people, mostly Tutsi people, were murdered in Rwanda. Massacres and persecution of both Tutsi and Hutu people have continued in Rwanda and neighbouring Burundi. Many have fled from their homes.

Rwanda
Burundi

Somalia
Refugees have been fleeing Somalia since 1988. Many have fled to Europe as well as other African countries. Many have stayed in Somalia but have lost their homes. About 200,000 were displaced within Somalia in 2000.

R u s s i a

Eastern Europe
In the 1990s there was fighting in southern
Russia, Armenia, Azerbaijan and Georgia.
There were nearly two million displaced people
in this area by 2001. In Chechnya the demands
for independence from Russian rule led to
military attacks on Chechnya by Russian troops.

Iran
Abuses of human rights in Iran have
caused many Iranians to flee and seek
sanctuary elsewhere. Iranians who
oppose the Islamic government have
been unlawfully imprisoned, tortured,
and executed. The same has happened
to students and other young people
who have demonstrated against
restrictions to free speech, including
the closing down of newspapers.

Afghanistan
Since the start of the war in Afghanistan
in 1972 many have had to leave their
homes. The majority has found sanctuary
in neighbouring Iran, which had 1.4 million
Afghan refugees in 2001 and in Pakistan,
which had 1.2 million in 2001. They are
the biggest refugee group in Britain.

China

Afghanistan

Pakistan

China
Asylum seekers from China and Tibet
have come to Europe seeking refuge
from abuses of their human rights.
Chinese citizens do not have full
freedom of speech, as well as lacking
other democratic rights. They cannot
criticise the Government without fear
of imprisonment and possible
execution. Since 1950, the Chinese
army has occupied Tibet, denying
its citizens human rights including
freedom of worship.

India

India and Pakistan
Both were put on Britain's
list of 'safe' countries in 1996
but there have been many
complaints of abuses of
human rights from these
countries, including torture
by police officers. In 1997
Pardeep Saini, flew from
India to Britain clinging onto
the landing wheels of an
aeroplane. His application
for asylum was refused.

Sri Lanka

Sri Lanka
There is a war in Sri Lanka
between some of the Tamil
minority, who want independence,
and the Sri Lankan government
and army. Refugees from the war
have fled to Britain and other
European countries, as well as
India and Canada.

Why do we remember Stephen Lawrence?

In April 1993 a teenager called Stephen Lawrence was murdered in a racist attack. Nobody has ever been convicted of his murder. An official inquiry into the murder and the police investigation that followed it concluded that incompetence and racism among the London Metropolitan Police Service had prevented justice. The case of Stephen Lawrence led to far reaching recommendations affecting the law, local government, education, and the National Health Service.

What happened to Stephen Lawrence on 22 April 1993?

Stephen Lawrence was an ordinary eighteen-year-old, studying for his A levels and hoping to train as an architect in the future. On 22 April he was returning home with a friend when he was brutally murdered. Stephen was black and his attackers were white. The following extract is from the Report of the Macpherson Inquiry (February 1999), the official inquiry into Stephen's murder. It was led by Sir William Macpherson.

The whole incident which led to his murder probably lasted no more than 15–20 seconds. Stephen Lawrence had been with his friend Duwayne Brooks during the afternoon of 22 April. They were on their way home when they came at around 22:30 to the bus stop in Well Hall Road. Stephen went to see if a bus was coming, and reached a position almost in the centre of the mouth of Dickson Road. Mr Brooks was part of the way between Dickson Road and the roundabout when he saw the group of five or six white youths who were responsible for Stephen's death on the opposite side of the road.

Mr Brooks called out to ask if Stephen saw the bus coming. One of the youths must have heard something said, since he called out: 'what, what nigger?' With that the group came quickly across the road and literally engulfed Stephen. During this time one or more of the group stabbed Stephen twice. Mr Brooks then turned and ran and called out to Stephen to run and to follow him.

Three eyewitnesses were at the bus stop. None of these witnesses was able later to identify any of the suspects.

All of them said that the attack was sudden and short. The group of white murderers then disappeared down Dickson Road.

Mr Brooks ran across the road in the direction of Shooters Hill, and he was followed by his friend Stephen Lawrence, who managed somehow to get to his feet and to run over 100 yards to the point where he fell. That place is now marked with a granite memorial stone set into the pavement.

Stephen had been stabbed to a depth of about five inches on both sides of the front of his body to the chest and arm. No great quantities of blood marked the scene of the attack or the track taken by Stephen, because he wore five layers of clothing. But when he fell he was bleeding freely, and nearly all of the witnesses who saw him lying there speak of a substantial quantity of blood.

The medical evidence indicates that Stephen was dead before he was removed by the ambulance men some time later. The amount of blood which had been lost would have made it probable that Stephen died where he fell on the pavement, and probably within a short time of his fall.

From the Macpherson Report (February 1999)

Why has the Stephen Lawrence case been called a miscarriage of justice?

Although the police received important information from the public soon after the murder, no one has ever been convicted of the murder of Stephen Lawrence. Stephen's family, in desperation, took the men they believed to be guilty to court themselves but failed to convict them of murder. The Government then ordered an inquiry into why justice had not been done for the Lawrences and how racial crimes should be investigated in future. This was the Macpherson Inquiry. The findings of the Macpherson Inquiry shocked the British public. They were widely reported and discussed in the press and media. Sir Paul Condon, Metropolitan Police Commissioner, apologised for 'our failure' to the Lawrence family although he did not accept an important conclusion of the inquiry

– that the police force was 'institutionally racist'.

What is 'institutional racism'?

'Institutional racism' means that racism is built into the systems and cultures of organisations – in other words – racism forms part of the way people are encouraged to think, behave and act.

What were the main findings of the Macpherson Report?

The Macpherson Report concluded that the Metropolitan Police Service – along with the wider Criminal Justice System (the law, law courts, prisons and probation service) – was 'institutionally racist'. In other words, police officers, as well as law courts and prisons, racially discriminated against minority ethnic groups. The Metropolitan Police Service was also, according to the Report, guilty of incompetence and poor leadership. This racism, incompetence and poor leadership prevented the police from being able to solve Stephen's murder and from being able to treat his family with respect and sensitivity. The main findings were that:

- Doreen and Neville Lawrence [Stephen Lawrence's parents] were treated insensitively and thoughtlessly. They were patronised, insulted and not kept informed about what was going on.
- Duwayne Brookes was also treated badly by the police and without respect or sensitivity. This racist attitude to Duwayne Brooks hampered the investigation. For example, police ignored his description, confirmed by others, that one attacker was fair-haired.
- Racist attitudes and stereotyping led police officers to assume immediately that there had been a fight between Stephen and Duwayne despite the reports of eyewitnesses. Some police officers could not accept it was a racist murder even after interviewing eyewitnesses.
- Police failed to follow up leads on suspects, interview suspects, carry out house-to-house searches or interview friends and associates of

suspects despite getting valuable information from the public very soon after the murder.

- Police failed to give Stephen first aid at the scene.
- Notes were not properly kept of the investigation, witnesses or informants.
- Members of the public who came forward with information were badly treated and not adequately protected.
- Arrests of suspects and house searches were delayed until 7 May for no good reason.
- House searches were poorly done. Witnesses had told police that knives were hidden under floorboards but police failed to lift the floorboards and search underneath.
- Police officers in charge of the investigation allowed it 'to drift'; failing to follow up leads or pass around information.
- Identification parades and surveillance of suspects were both badly carried out.
- Some police officers used racist language such as 'Negro' and 'coloured'. According to the Report: 'Racism awareness training was almost non-existent at every level'.

So many errors, the Report concluded, could not be explained by incompetence alone but by racism as well. In other words, if the victim had been white and the suspects had been black, the police would have behaved differently.

Race equality after Macpherson?

In total, the Macpherson Report made seventy recommendations. These recommendations were made in order to promote racial equality within the police service and British society as a whole. The Report recommended that the police service should give anti-racist training to officers and make a special effort to get more people from minority ethnic groups to join it. The Report also recommended that the police service should be inspected in a similar way to how OFSTED inspects schools. These inspections would check that the police service is tackling racism in a positive way. The Report defined racism as 'any incident or action that is seen as racist by the victim or any other person'. It said that this definition should be adopted by schools and the National Health Service as well as by the police service. Three of the recommendations were to do with education and are shown in **Source A**.

Source A

67. Changes should be made to the National Curriculum. The National Curriculum must show that it values everyone in society and it must help to stop racism. It must be suitable for a society with different ethnic groups.

68. Local Education Authorities and School Governors must take action to stop racism in schools. These actions must include:
    - schools recording all racist incidents;
    - all recorded incidents must be reported to the pupils' parents/guardians, School Governors and LEAs;
    - the numbers of racist incidents must be published annually by each school;
    - the numbers and ethnic identity of 'excluded' pupils to be published annually by each school.

69. That OFSTED inspections must check that the school is taking action against racism.

Recommendations 67–69 adapted from the Macpherson Report, related to education. From http://www.official-documents.co.uk/document/cm42/4262/sli-47.htm#r1

The Report also recommended that the laws against racism should be improved and strengthened. As a result, the Race Relations Amendment Act was passed in April 2001. Instead of hoping that organisations will be anti-racist – the Act makes them legally responsible for being anti-racist. This was an important change to previous laws about race relations and anti-racism.

The Race Relations Amendment Act (2001) said that:
- Organisations and public bodies e.g. the police, schools, and hospitals, must introduce positive anti-racist strategies. For example, they must monitor how many people from minority ethnic groups join the police service.
- Organisations and public bodies must consider their effect on racial equality. In other words – are they helping British society to be equal? How are they doing this?
- Inspectors will check that the police are meeting their anti-racist targets.

Source B

For a long time I have talked about education as the key... If those who murdered my son had been better educated... they would have realised that everything in this country has black people who have played a part in it.

Doreen Lawrence (From blink.org.uk.)

Stephen Lawrence's was an unusual case because it became very famous, not because a racist murder was unusual. In fact, Stephen was one of three victims of racist murders in Greenwich alone. In 2001 a report called 'Counting the Cost' found that there had been nineteen deaths from racially motivated attacks since the publication of the Macpherson Report in February 1999. It is clear, therefore, that Britain must take even more positive action to stop racially motivated violence and crime.

1 Read **Source B**. Do you agree with Doreen Lawrence that education is the key to tackling racism and racist discrimination?

2 Read **Source A**. How does your school promote racial equality?

3 In Chapter 12 you found out about the Scarman Report. Compare the main conclusions to those of the Macpherson Report.
What are the differences?
What reasons can you suggest for these differences?

The case of Stephen Lawrence has been compared to the case of Rodney King in Los Angeles, America in 1992.
Find out what happened in the case of Rodney King. In what ways was it similar to the case of Stephen Lawrence?

What are the issues of living in a multicultural society?

The purpose of this chapter is to stimulate discussion about the key issues in Britain today about life within a multicultural society. How can an understanding of the history of immigration and settlement be valuable now? What can be done to ensure that Britain becomes a peaceful and united multicultural society?

Cultural diversity A phrase used to convey the belief that people are different but equal and that the differences are a cause for celebration.

How has Britain been enriched by the cultural diversity of its people?

The diversity of British people both in the past and today has contributed greatly to our culture and had an important impact on all areas of British life, including language, music, architecture, food, trade, industry, business, politics and so on. Most of the time these influences are so central to our way of life that we fail to recognise that they come from immigration and settlement. There is, for example, the Norman influence on language and government in the Middle Ages, the Italian influence on music and architecture from the sixteenth century onwards, and the imperial influence on all aspects of life in the nineteenth and twentieth centuries. **Sources A** and **B** are pictures of a building on Fournier Street in the East End of London. This building has changed over time and these changes reflect patterns of immigration into Britain.

Look back to the map of the East End in Chapter 3. Find Fournier Street in Spitalfields. **Source A** is a photograph of a mosque on Fournier Street in 1993. The building has not always been a mosque. In 1743 the first religious building on this site was the 'Neuve Eglise' or New Church, built for French Huguenots (Protestants) who came to Spitalfields to escape religious persecution in France. In Spitalfields, Huguenot refugees made important contributions to the local silk-weaving industry. From 1809 until 1898 the building was used as a Methodist chapel. Many Methodists were Welsh people who came to the East End because of poverty and a lack of job opportunities in Wales. In 1898 the chapel became a synagogue for the local Jewish population, many of whom had fled pogroms in Eastern Europe. **Source B** shows the inside of the synagogue. By the 1960s, however, the Jewish population in the area had fallen in number. In 1976, the building became a mosque, reflecting the immigration of large numbers of Asians, particularly from Bangladesh, into the area in the 1960s.

Source A

Source B

What are the responsibilities of leaders, including politicians, within a multicultural society?

As you have found out in Chapters 10, 11 and 13, politicians have sometimes played the 'race card' to try to win votes in local and general elections. In the run up to the general election of 2001, politicians were accused of playing the race card. In March 2001, at the Conservative Party Conference, the leader of the Party, William Hague, said: 'Let me take you on a journey to a foreign land – to Britain after a second term of Tony Blair [and the Labour Party]'. Hague denied that he was talking about the effect of immigration on British culture. However, following Hague's speech, John Townend, a Conservative MP, said that 'Anglo-Saxon culture' had been 'seriously undermined by immigration' and that the British were becoming a 'mongrel race'.

Bill Morris, the black leader of the Transport and General Workers Union, responded to Hague by saying: 'To many of us, it is indeed a foreign land. A foreign land where ordinary black British families wake up almost every morning to listen on the radio to descriptions of themselves that they do not recognise'. Bill Morris went on to say that he was more frightened of racist politicians than of racists on the street, because 'the words of our politicians are sometimes taken by the racists as a licence to attack anyone who does not look and speak like them'. In April 2001 the London Metropolitan Police Service released figures that confirmed Bill Morris's fears – in the week after William Hague's speech the number of racist attacks in Britain doubled.

The Labour Party was also criticised for its attitude towards minority ethnic groups in the run up to the 2001 general election. Twelve new candidates from minority ethnic groups stood in the election for the Labour Party but 10 of these 12 were given constituencies with large Conservative majorities. It was very unlikely, therefore, that any of these 10 candidates would win their seats. During the 1980s there were more black and Asian Labour candidates and more black and Asian Labour councillors than there were at the beginning of the twenty-first century.

Source C

Criticisms of William Hague and John Townend were also made by Lord Taylor, a black Conservative peer within the House of Lords. Taylor, a barrister and presenter of radio and television programmes about legal issues, was made a lord in 1997. His outspoken criticism of the racism of some MPs within his own party helped force two of them to apologise in the run up to the 2001 general election.

Q

1 Look at **Source D**:
   a) What is the 'Tory Party' referred to in the cartoon?
   b) What is the meaning of what the wolf is saying?
   c) Why is the wolf disguised as a sheep?
   d) How does this cartoon help us to understand issues around race and culture in the twenty-first century?

Source D

From the Observer newspaper, 22 April 2001.

Britain: a changing nation?

Issues of immigration, settlement and cultural diversity continue to be topical issues. **Source E** shows some statistics about Britain from the national census of 1991.

Source E

5.5% of the British population was from a minority ethnic group.

1.5% was Indian.

0.9% was black Caribbean.

0.9% was Pakistani.

0.4% was black African.

Census 1991

Look at **Source E**:

a) Why is it important to ask about ethnic origin in a census?

b) Find out about the results of the 2001 census. The www.statistics.gov.uk Internet site has statistics from the census and elsewhere.

c) What changes do you notice in the ethnic origin of the British population since 1991?

d) What reasons can you suggest for these changes?

1 What are the issues for politicians in a multicultural society?

2 Some pressure groups have argued that politicians should not be allowed to use racist language. In small groups, draw up a 'Code of Conduct' for behaviour by politicians.

3 Why might some politicians object to having a 'Code of Conduct'? Do you think politicians should agree to a 'Code of Conduct'? Use **Source D**, as well as other information from this book, to support and develop your arguments.

4 What do you think should be the role of education within a multicultural society?

Coursework activity

The following questions could form all or part of a GCSE coursework assignment.

1 With reference to the period 1880 to the present day, explain why people chose to emigrate to Britain?

2 With reference to the period 1880 to the present day, explain the main challenges faced by immigrants starting a new life in Britain?

3 'From a study of British history it is possible to question the widespread vision of Britain as a country characterised by a spirit of toleration.'

Adapted from the book *A Tolerant Country?* (1991) by Colin Holmes, a Professor of History.

From your studies, and using information from this book, how far do you agree that Britain has been a tolerant nation?

What is your identity?

In April 1990 Norman Tebbit, a Conservative MP, said that it would be an 'interesting test' to see how many British Asians cheered on the teams from the country of their ethnic origin rather than England at cricket. His remarks upset many within the British Asian community who felt that Tebbit was saying that they did not see themselves as British. **Sources F** to **H** are the words of teenagers talking about their own sense of identity in the 1990s.

Graham Gooch and Devon Malcolm of England discuss tactics during a test match against the West Indies.

Source F

My mother tongue is Bengali but it's not true to say I can speak Bengali. I don't really consider Bangladesh as home. I've spent my entire life here in England... but I've always been classified as Bengali born in Britain. Many occasions have arisen where I have been purposely ignored and deliberately made to feel left out...

Ataul Choudhury

Source G

I am a bilingual person who speaks English and Bengali. Bengali is very important for me, because it's my own language. When I think of the day when many Bengali people died for their own language, I say to myself, 'If our own people died to keep their own language, then I'll sacrifice any other languages to keep my own'. I am proud that I speak two languages. I am proud of our language, it's who I am, it's part of me.

Hazera Begum

Source H

During my life I have changed friends and schools quite a few times. My strongest memory of these times is when I left Bromley Hall School to come to Homerton House [a secondary school in Hackney, London]. The thing I remember most is the way the kids used different forms of slang. I used phrases like 'chill out man', 'clap it' meaning 'shut up' and, 'hold your corner' meaning stay where you are. None of the boys understood what I was talking about... Once I arrived at Homerton House I knew things would be different. The day I arrived, my friend Roland met me at the gate, he said 'Ade, you're safe man!'

Adrian Southwell

Q

2 **Sources F** and **G** have different attitudes to identity. What are the differences?

3 What issues are raised about life in multicultural Britain by all three sources?

Activity

We all, whatever our ethnic origin, have a sense of identity. Our identity can be formed in many different ways – from our regional culture, our gender, our religion, social class, political beliefs, generation/age, popular culture and so on. Use this list and any other areas that you can think of to explore and reach some conclusions about your own identity.

INDEX